LJB

09 2006

D0096691

LONELY PLANET
ROAD TRIP

BLUE RIDGE PARKWAY

Loretta Chilcoat

Road Trip Blue Ridge Parkway
1st edition – May 2005

Published by Lonely Planet Publications Pty Ltd
ABN 36 005 607 983

Australia	Head Office, Locked Bag 1, Footscray, Vic 3011
	☎ 03 8379 8000 fax 03 8379 8111
	🖳 talk2us@lonelyplanet.com.au
USA	150 Linden St, Oakland, CA 94607
	☎ 510 893 8555 toll free 800 275 8555
	fax 510 893 8572
	🖳 info@lonelyplanet.com
UK	72–82 Rosebery Avenue, London EC1R 4RW
	☎ 020 7841 9000 fax 020 7841 9001
	🖳 go@lonelyplanet.co.uk

This title was commissioned in Lonely Planet's Oakland office and produced by: **Commissioning Editor & Project Manager** Kathleen Munnelly **Series & Cover Designer** Candice Jacobus **Regional Publishing Manager** David Zingarelli

Freelancers: Cartographer Bart Wright **Layout Designer** Hayley Tsang **Editor** Valerie Sinzdak **Indexer** Ken DellaPenta **Proofer** Michele Posner

© Lonely Planet Publications Pty Ltd 2005.

All rights reserved.

Cover photograph Mabry Mill in Virginia, David Muench/CORBIS. All images are copyright of the photographers unless otherwise indicated.

ISBN 1 74059 939 X

Printed through The Bookmaker International Ltd.
Printed in China

Lonely Planet and the Lonely Planet logo are trademarks of Lonely Planet and are registered in the US Patent and Trademark Office and in other countries.

Lonely Planet does not allow its name or logo to be appropriated by commercial establishments, such as retailers, restaurants or hotels. Please let us know of any misuses: 🖳 www.lonelyplanet.com/ip

Although the authors and Lonely Planet have taken all reasonable care in preparing this book, we make no warranty about the accuracy or completeness of its content and, to the maximum extent permitted, disclaim all liability arising from its use.

CONTENTS

The closest major airports are **Washington Dulles International** (IAD; ☎ 703-572-2700; www.metwashairports.com/dulles) and **Ronald Reagan Washington National** (DCA; ☎ 703-417-8000; www. metwashairports.com/national) in the northern section. Smaller airports like **Asheville Regional** (AVL; www.flyavl.com), **Charlottesville–Albemarle Regional** (CHO; ☎ 434-973-8342), **Roanoke Regional** (RIC; ☎ 540-362-1999; www.roanokeregionalairport.com) and **Shenandoah Valley Regional** (SHD; ☎ 540-234-8304) also serve the area.

Most rental-car agencies have stations at both large and small airports. They require a credit card and proof you're older than 25 (or they'll tack on a hefty surcharge). The major agencies include **Alamo** (☎ 800-327-9633; www.alamo.com), **Avis** (☎ 800-321-3712l; www.avis.com), **Budget** (☎ 800-527-0700; www.budget.com), **Dollar** (☎ 800-800-4000; www.dollar.com), **Hertz** (☎ 800-654-3131; www. hertz.com), **National** (☎ 800-328-4567; www.nationalcar.com) and **Thrifty** (☎ 800-367-2277; www.thrifty.com).

There is no bus service to the Parkway. The following towns, in order from north to south, are served by **Greyhound** (☎ 800-229-9424; www.greyhound.com): Charlottesville, Waynesboro, Staunton, Buena Vista, Lynchburg, Roanoke, Hillsville, Galax, Boone and Asheville. A typical fare from Washington, DC, to Waynesboro, Virginia (the start of the Blue Ridge Parkway), is $40; the trip takes four hours and 45 minutes. Car rental is available in Charlottesville, Lynchburg, Roanoke and Asheville.

For travelers with older cars, the ups and downs of this trip could wreak a little havoc on your transmission. Consider purchasing 24-hour roadside assistance from **AAA** (American Automobile Association; ☎ 800-874-7532; www.aaa.com) in addition to your regular coverage.

If you want to explore the Parkway behind the giant wheel of an RV, rent one from **Cruise America** (☎ 800-671-8042; www.cruiseamerica.com), and remember the unwritten etiquette rule of pulling off at an overlook if there are more than five cars behind you.

Bicycling

The Parkway is a great route for avid bicyclists, especially with its low speed limit and absence of commercial vehicles. However, it was primarily designed for motorized travel, and several developed areas are spaced too far apart for comfortable travel by bicycle, particularly campgrounds. Cyclists should then seek shelter and facilities off the Parkway, but be warned that roads leaving the Parkway can be quite steep (particularly around Floyd, Virginia, and NC 80 in North Carolina).

Endurance and preparation are key, as traveling the length of the Parkway involves an elevation change of more than 48,000ft (equivalent to roughly 9 vertical miles), with the lowest point at 600ft and the highest at 6000ft.

Bicycles are not permitted on trails or walkways. Riders should travel single file (except when passing or turning left) and well to the right-hand side of the road. Bikes should be equipped with a white light or reflector visible from at least 500ft in the front and a red light or reflector visible from at least 200ft in the rear during periods of low visibility, between the hours of sunset and sunrise, or when traveling through a tunnel. You must maintain (and not exceed) a speed that's consistent with weather conditions and other traffic.

To make sure your bike trip is as safe as possible, wear a bicycle helmet at all times; carry a first-aid and tire-repair kit; wear breathable, high-visibility clothes in layers; pack extra water and high-energy snacks; and avoid the Parkway during foggy conditions. For information before your trip, or to check current weather conditions, contact the **Superintendent's Office** (☎ 828-298-0398; Blue Ridge Parkway, 199 Hemphill Knob Rd, Asheville, NC 28803).

You might also want to consider the more than 900 miles of traffic-free trails and 2000 miles of paved, gravel and dirt roads in the George Washington National Forest. Biking is especially popular in the Pisgah National Forest. For more detailed information on routes and tours, check out the Blue Ridge Bicycle Club in Asheville, North Carolina (www.blueridgebicycleclub.org), and in Roanoke, Virginia (www.blueridgebicycleclub.com).

A final word of caution: Strongly consider using a flashlight in the Parkway's 26 tunnels as some of them have severe curves and are pitch black even with car headlights (tunnels are not illuminated).

Orientation

Travel along the Blue Ridge Parkway is marked by 'mileposts,' which are stumpy, wooden posts and/or concrete markers on the side of the road. Each one is numbered from north-south in increments of one mile, and all sights and attractions in this guide have directions listed according to the nearest milepost (ie, MP 64).

ITINERARIES

Driving the Parkway north to south is the most popular way of experiencing the road, so that's how this book is organized. The following itineraries detail the granddaddy of all trips (doing it all at once), plus some weekend-long options in the most popular areas.

THE CLASSIC: TWO WEEKS

Give yourself at least two weeks to drive this 469-mile megaroute, taking time to leave the Parkway occasionally and explore the towns and cities that have been shaped and influenced by the road.

Starting from the northern end in Waynesboro, Virginia, head south, stopping off at **Sherando Lake** and various overlooks until bedding down at **Peaks of Otter**. The next day, detour off to **Bedford** before exploring the **Roanoke** area and spen ding the night there. On day three you've got some ground to cover, jamming at the **Floyd Country Store** before camping out at **Rocky Knob**.

Get up early for buckwheat pancakes at **Mabry Mill** and then move into North Carolina and a hike in the **Doughton Park** area. Sleep it off at **Bluff Mountain** before saddling up in **Blowing Rock** and touring the Flat Top Manor at **Moses H Cone Memorial Park** on horseback. Enjoy a luxurious rest at **Chetola Resort** in Blowing Rock or a night under the stars at **Julian Price Memorial Park**.

Spend the day hiking at **Grandfather Mountain** or along **Linville Falls** before heading to **Burnsville** for a relaxing sleep on a bona-fide dude ranch. The next day, jump back on the Parkway and retrace your steps a little at **Crabtree Meadows** before catching an unforgettable sunset at the highest point on the Parkway, **Mt Mitchell State Park**. Spend the night in **Black Mountain**.

Check out the ethereal view from **Craggy Gardens Visitor Center** before shopping at the **Folk Art Center** and then moving on to **Asheville** for a few nights in one of its famed B&Bs. On your last day in Asheville, tour the **Biltmore Estate** before moving south to the **Pisgah Inn** for a high-altitude sleepover. Get your strength back for some water fun at **Graveyard Fields** or **Sliding Rock** before heading south toward the end of the Parkway in Cherokee.

WEEKEND BREAKS

PEAKS OF OTTER AREA
Grab a late breakfast at the Peaks of Otter restaurant and spend the afternoon on the **Fallingwater Cascades Loop** trail that winds through part of the George Washington & Jefferson National Forest.

Pay homage to fallen heroes at the **National D-Day Memorial** in Bedford. Stay overnight at the **Peaks of Otter Lodge**.

ROANOKE AREA
Spend the morning on **Roanoke Mountain**, then take the kids to the

Kid Stuff

- **Mill Mountain Zoo** (p22): High-altitude encounters with reptiles and monkeys
- **Mabry Mill** (p24): Live demonstrations of blacksmithing and soap-making along a living history walking trail
- **Altapass Orchard** (p43): Apple pickin', storytellin' and hayridin' in the mountains
- **Tweetsie Railroad** (p34): Chug-a-luggin' on pint-size cars for pint-size people
- **Sliding Rock** (p57): Mother Nature's chilly waterslide on a long, slippery boulder
- **Graveyard Fields** (p58): A fun, easy hike with rewarding splash areas along the way
- **Mile-High Swinging Bridge** (p39): Fearless kids bounding across steel planks

Camping on the Parkway

There are nine campgrounds along the Parkway. Four are in Virginia: Otter Creek (MP 61), Peaks of Otter (MP 86), Roanoke Mountain (MP 120.4) and Rocky Knob (MP 167). Five are in North Carolina: Doughton Park (MP 241.1), Price Park (MP 296.9), Linville Falls (MP 316), Crabtree Meadows (MP 339.5) and Mt Pisgah (MP 408.8). They are all open from May to October, except Linville Falls, which is open year-round. Reservations are accepted in advance for Linville Falls and Price Park only through **ReserveUSA** (☎ 877-444-6777; www.reserveusa.com); all others are available on a first-come, first-served basis.

Campground fees are $14 for families or groups with two adults, plus $2 for each extra person 18 or older. There are no hookups or showers. Along the Parkway, you'll find seven picnic grounds in developed areas, plus tables at some of the overlooks.

Mill Mountain Zoo and/or **Virginia Explore Park**. Go into town for lunch in **Center in the Square**

Take an early evening trek back up the mountain for a sunset hike to the glowing, landmark **Roanoke Star**. Stay the night in the **Roanoke Hotel**.

ASHEVILLE AREA

After a filling gourmet breakfast at your B&B, spend the day exploring the luxurious **Biltmore Estate**.

In the evening, enjoy a truly organic treat at **The Market Place**. Return to your B&B for a sumptuous sleep before grabbing an early coffee at **Blue Moon Bakery** the following day. Get out on the water or explore some underwater caves with one of the regional outfitters before having a bite at **Max and Rosie's** and another perfect sleep in true southern style.

HIGHLIGHTS

Sherando Lake (p14) Enjoy a family-friendly beach picnic in the shadow of mountains.

Blue Ridge Music Center (p27) Learn all you ever wanted to know about the twangy genre.

Altapass Orchard (p43) Come for the pickin' (apples and banjoes) and the prime views of the Blue Ridge.

Grandfather Mountain (p39) Fulfill your Indiana Jones fantasy crossing the mile-high swinging bridge, and test your endurance on challenging hiking trails.

Mt Mitchell State Park (p45) Catch some serious air at the highest point of the Parkway and, if the fog cooperates, take in the best sunset this side of the Mississippi.

Asheville (p48) Visit a true southern lady of the south, with exceptional architecture and lavish B&Bs.

VIRGINIA

The Parkway stretches for 209 country miles in Virginia, paralleling fantastic recreational lake areas, meandering by world-class bluegrass venues and passing through the vibrant city of Roanoke. It might not have the same caliber of alpine vistas as the North Carolina portion, but don't knock the bucolic farmland that can suddenly open to a panoramic spread shutterbugs clamor for. It would take about five hours to drive this section of the Parkway without stopping, from Humpback Rocks to Cumberland Knob, but who wants to do that? This is a 'scenic' drive, so allow plenty of time for stopping at overlooks and snapping that perfect Kodak moment.

The Parkway's **North Entrance** is rather unremarkable – mostly due to its location: a rundown intersection of I-64, US 250 and an abandoned visitor center-gas station. But don't let this tarnish your view of this majestic, all-American road. Trust us, it gets much better than this.

WAYNESBORO

Population 20,000; Map 7

Settled in 1797 by Irish and German immigrants and named after a Revolutionary War hero, General 'Mad' Anthony Wayne, Waynesboro offers a few sights to see, but the town is best known as the place where Skyline Drive and the Blue Ridge Parkway come together. It's a convenient place to fuel up, chow down and get a good night's sleep before journeying further. Waynesboro is 8 miles east of the junction of I-81 and I-64.

The **P Buckley Moss Museum** (☎ 540-949-6473; 150 P Buckley Moss Dr; admission free; ⊙ 10am-6pm Mon-Sat, 12:30-5:30pm Sun) is dedicated to Moss, very much a 'people's artist,' whose subject matter includes the Amish and Mennonite communities. From I-64, take exit 94; turn left onto US 340 and drive a block or so.

There are also four galleries in the **Shenandoah Valley Art Center** (☎ 540-942-7662; 600 W Main St; admission free; ⊙ 10am-4pm Tue-Sat, 2-4pm Sun).

For more information on attractions, contact the **Waynesboro Tourism Office** (☎ 540-942-6644; 301 W Main St; ⊙ 8am-5pm Mon-Fri). There is a **visitor center** (☎ 540-943-5187; ⊙ 10am-6pm Mon-Sat) at Afton Mountain (exit 99 off I-64).

SLEEPING & EATING

SHENANDOAH ACRES RESORT

☎ 540-337-1911; www.shenacres.com; County Rd 660; campsite/camper cabin/cottage $22/50/107; ⊙ May-Sep; ☒

With miniature golf, playground equipment in the water, basketball and volleyball, this campy leisure land keeps kids easily amused, although beach parties and DJ dancing also draw singles and nonfamily travelers. Check the website to view your tent or cottage sleeping arrangements in advance. The **swimming area** (adult/child 6-11 weekdays $7.25/5, weekends $9.25/5.75) is open to the public. From the Parkway, take VA 664 west to VA 610 west; proceed for a half mile and turn left onto Lake Rd.

AFTON HOUSE
☎ 877-214-8133; www.aftonhouse.com; r/cottage $85-95/300-400; ☒

The original inn served as an 1860s summer resort but burned down in 1963. Fortunately, the present B&B is just as charming and close to the Parkway. From I-64, take exit 99 (Afton-Waynesboro), then US 250 east to VA 6 east. Follow VA 6 less than a half mile to the Afton House.

IRIS INN
☎ 888-585-9018; www.irisinn.com; 191 Chinquapin Dr; d $95-125

This modern mountain retreat draws guests with its spacious great room and roaring fireplace (perfect for those chilly evenings). Take in vast views of the Shenandoah Valley from the lookout tower. There is a room equipped for disabled guests.

SHORTY'S DINER
☎ 540-885-8861; 1013 Richmond Ave; dishes $5-15; ⏰ 7am-9pm Sun-Thu, to 10pm Fri & Sat

Bottomless sweet tea and cakes and pies bigger than a breadbox make for good Southern eats at this spot with chessboard floors.

DETOUR: MONTICELLO

East of Charlottesville, Thomas Jefferson's magnificent **home** (☎ 434-984-9800; adult/child 6-11 $13/6; ⏰ Mar 1-Oct 31 8am-5pm, Nov 1-Feb 28 9am-4:30pm), featured on the nickel coin, embodies its resident-designer: Jefferson's quirky inventions and French-inspired innovations are scattered throughout. His tomb is downhill; its inscription was chosen by the man himself. Daily specialty tours include a Plantation Community tour exposing the complicated past of the slave owner whose most famous work (the *Declaration of Independence*) proclaimed all men to be equal.

Keep in mind that Monticello (mon-ta-**chel**-o) is one of Virginia's premier historic attractions; arrive early to avoid long lines. Frequent shuttles run from the parking lot up the hill. Tours are also offered at the nearby 1784 **Michie Tavern** (☎ 434-977-1234), which also serves heaping buffets of Southern grub in **The Ordinary** (around $15), and at James Monroe's 535-acre estate, **Ash Lawn–Highland** (☎ 434-293-9539; adult/child 6-11 $9/5), 2½ miles east of Monticello. A combo ticket for all three ('Presidents' Pass') is $25, available at either attraction or from the **Charlottesville–Albemarle Convention & Visitors Bureau** (☎ 434-977-1783; www.charlottesvilletourism.org; VA 20S near I-64 exit 121A).

Take the Parkway to I-64 east; get off at Exit 121A and follow signs to Monticello.

To get there, go west on Main St, which becomes US 250 (Jefferson Hwy), and drive toward Staunton.

WEASIE'S KITCHEN
☎ 540-943-0500; 130 E Broad St; dishes under $10
Inexpensive lunches and dinners, plus rib-sticking breakfasts served all day, will fuel your belly and get you movin' on up to the Parkway.

HUMPBACK ROCKS
Map 2; MP 5.8
Humpback Rocks is the first visitor center on the Parkway, with a small exhibit on mountain life in the 19th century and an over-worked air-conditioning system that keeps the place just above freezing. There's an easy, self-guided trail about the surrounding geology and plant life that departs from the visitor center.

A tremendously scaled-back version of Williamsburg, Virginia, the **Mountain Farm Trail** (☎ 540-377-2377) is a reconstructed farmstead featuring a trail past stone buildings with interactive demonstrations in the summer (in other months, the trail is self-guided). Kids will especially enjoy climbing, scrambling and poking around the chicken coop, log cabin and honey tree while learning about quilting, basket-weaving and preparing homemade foods over an open-hearth fire – they'll also thank their lucky stars for microwaves.

ON THE ROAD
For a moderate hike and access to the **Appalachian Trail** (AT), stop at MP 6 and head 1 mile straight up to the smooth, rounded peaks (hence the name) of Humpback Rocks, where you'll see a hazy, 360° view of Rockfish and Shenandoah valleys below. The path is quick and steep, but allow about an hour if you're a novice climber.

The road meanders through open farmland and tunnels of canopied trees for the next few miles. Ahead, the moderate **Greenstone Trail** (MP 8.8) leaves from the Greenstone parking area. This short, 0.2-mile nature trail loops through an old oak and hickory forest, as well as greenstone rock formations, giving hikers a glimpse of the geology of the northern Blue Ridge Mountains.

At MP 10.7, stop at the **Ravens Roost Overlook** for a sweeping vista of Torry Mountain and the Shenandoah Valley. You might also catch a glimpse of a hang-glider since this is one of three launch sites along the Parkway.

Take the VA 664E exit at Reeds Gap (between MP 13 and 14) for about a mile to get to **Wintergreen Resort** (☎ 800-266-2444; www.wintergreenresort.com; d summer/winter $154-181/126-199). This full-service resort features downhill ski slopes (see 'The White Stuff,' p30), restaurants, a bar, outdoor pools, an indoor pool, tennis courts, 45 golf holes, hiking trails, a riding center, an exercise room and sauna, and the 20-acre Lake Monocan for swimming and canoeing. A short drive from the main hall (there's shuttle service) are cushy condos, many of which have Jacuzzi tubs, wood-burning fireplaces and private balconies overlooking the ski runs. A staff biologist organizes interpretive walks among the more than 6000 acres of protected forest. All of this does not come cheap, though: A round of golf will cost $90 on weekdays and $100 on weekends, and fees apply for tennis, the Wintergarden spa (but oh, so worth it), guided mountain bike trips and horseback riding.

Just 4 miles off the Parkway at MP 16 (take VA 814), the family-friendly **Sherando Lake Recreation Area** (☎ 540-261-6105; vehicle with 1/2/3+ people $4/6/8, bicycle $1; campsite $15-20; ☽ Apr 1-Oct 31; ☏) is part of the George Washington & Jefferson National Forest. The 24-acre lake boasts a small beach and bathhouse, a visitor center and an open-air, stone fireplace for spooky tales and perfect s'mores. The family campsites are available on a first-come, first-served basis. The Cliff Trail takes hikers above the lake. You can also opt for a self-guided nature trail closer to the camping area.

For a pretty excursion through dense hemlock, try the **White Rock Falls Trail** (MP 19.9) a moderate 1.8-mile trail to a waterfall with a crystal-clear plunge pool. The trailhead starts at Slacks Overlook and ends at White Rock Gap (MP 18.5).

WHETSTONE RIDGE

Map 2; MP 29

If the term 'Grindstone Cowboy' leaps to mind when you're passing through **Whetstone Ridge**, it's probably because the name of this spot came from the sharpening stones used by mountain men near the ridge. Today you'll find a restaurant that specializes in hearty home cookin', plus restrooms and a pay phone.

A tiny, wooden marker denotes the entrance to the **Whetstone Ridge Trail**; from here South Mountain is 8 miles away and VA 603 is 11. Barren spots and tree skeletons remind hikers of the previous forest fire that consumed a small portion of the trail.

There's a pretty hike to **Crabtree Falls** (not to be confused with another Crabtree Falls in North Carolina at MP 339.5; see p44) about 6 miles off the Parkway on VA 56.

SLEEPING & EATING

CRABTREE FALLS CAMPGROUND

☎ 540-377-2066; 11039 Crabtree Falls Hwy in Tyro; campsite/camping cabin $18/50

The heated bathhouse, waterfront tent sites, megacool playground and Pac-Man machine in the game room make for a winning combination. You need to bring your own linens for the rustic cabins, but there's a small camp store for replenishing your s'mores supply. At MP 27, take VA 56 east for 7 miles; the campground is on the right.

WHETSTONE RIDGE RESTAURANT

☽ summer only

This small restaurant offers cheap burgers and fries and some of the best homemade soup. You'll see pretty views of the surrounding scenery, especially in early summer when blooms blanket the area.

ON THE ROAD

You'll probably notice from the NPS map that portions of the **George Washington & Jefferson National Forest** surround the Parkway from the North Entrance to MP 106, while another, larger section lies further west. Combined in 1995, these wonderfully remote forests provide ample opportunity to enjoy natural beauty the way the forefathers intended. Together, they stretch northeast to southwest across Virginia, spilling slightly into West Virginia and Kentucky and comprising a jaw-dropping 1.8 million miles of public land, one of the largest tracts in the eastern United States.

The US Department of Agriculture (USDA) Forest Service is the administrator of these national forests. The **Supervisor's Office**

Hiking the Appalachian Trail

The mighty Appalachian Trail is the mother of all footpaths. Running along the spine of the planet's most ancient mountain range, it weaves over 2174 miles from Springer Mountain, Georgia, to Mount Katahdin, Maine. Officially opened in 1937, it crosses 14 states, traveling up and down more than 350 mountain peaks above 5000ft, yet rarely ever leaves the wilderness. In its vast meandering, the AT (as most users call it) sneaks through one of the world's greatest forests, a dense constellation of fir, oak, maple, spruce, pine, birch, hemlock, ash, cedar and dogwood trees, just to name a few.

If you spend time on the AT, you might cross paths with two different breeds: 'through-hikers' and 'section hikers.' The former are the ones who go all the way, and every year about 2000 brave, determined and half-loony souls set out to attain that legendary status of an AT through-hiker. However, the vast majority of AT hikers fall under the second category, completing the trail piecemeal by selecting their times and locations to minimize difficulty.

The AT parallels roughly 108 miles of the Blue Ridge Parkway, from the northern entrance outside Waynesboro heading south to the N&W Railroad Overlook at MP 108. There are many opportunities to 'section-hike' portions of the trail from various overlooks, as a large number of Parkway trails overlap with the AT.

Today the AT is ruled over and cared for by the **Appalachian Trail Conference** (ATC, ☎ 304-535-6331; www.appalachiantrail.org) a nonprofit organization based in Harpers Ferry, West Virginia, which remains the ultimate resource for information on the trail.

If you're sufficiently inspired to take on the mighty AT, be sure to consult the ATC and make use of the group's extensive knowledge and many publications. Other useful books are Lonely Planet's *Hiking in the USA* and *Great Smoky Mountains & Shenandoah National Parks*; *Walking the Appalachian Trail* by Larry Luxemberg; *The Thru-Hiker's Handbook* by Dan 'Wingfoot' Bruce; *Beyond Backpacking: Ray Jardine's Guide to Lightweight Hiking*; and a hilarious take on the AT, Bill Bryson's *A Walk in the Woods*.

DETOUR: SURRENDER AT APPOMATTOX

On April 9, 1865 (Palm Sunday), in the modest house of Wilmer McLean at Appomattox Court House, Confederate general Robert E Lee, resplendent in his best uniform with his sword by his side, sat down to talk with Union general Ulysses S Grant, who was dressed in a private's tunic with lieutenant general's stars pinned to its shoulders. Traveller, Lee's horse, munched on the grass outside.

After a pause, Grant opened his notebook and in straightforward fashion spelled out the terms. These were generous and included mandates that would make it impossible to enact vengeance against former Confederate soldiers. After an exchange of military salutes, Lee returned to Traveller and rode away.

Grant sat down in front of his tent and reminisced about the Mexican War, not outwardly savoring the moment of victory. Lee rode past his troops, many of whom had tears streaming down their faces. In the following days the once-proud Army of Northern Virginia stacked up its arms, formally surrendered and wandered away to recommence their shattered lives.

Today the compact village is preserved within a 1300-acre park as **Appomattox Court House National Historic Park**, which houses a museum and NPS **visitor center** (☎ 434-352-8987; admission to grounds in season adult/child 16 & under $4/free, off-season $3/free; year-round). Within the evocative pedestrian-only village, you'll find 27 restored buildings, including **McLean House**. There's a clean **Super 8 Motel** (☎ 434-352-2339; r from $45) in town, and **Holliday Lake State Park** (☎ 804-248-6308; campsite/cabin from $14/90) offers seasonal camping nearby.

From the Parkway, take US 501 east (just past the James River Visitor Center) toward Lynchburg; then go east on US 460. When you reach Appomattox, take VA 24 north 2 miles to the courthouse.

(☎ 540-265-5100; www.southernregion.fs.fed.us/gwj; 5162 Valleypointe Pkwy, Roanoke, VA 24019) is the main headquarters; it provides good maps of the entire forest and detailed brochures.

From MP 27 you'll see just a handful of drop-off views of the surrounding valley as the road winds up and down. There aren't too many dramatic drop-offs along this stretch of the Parkway, and most overlooks and parking areas are heavily wooded. The views are just a short walk through the trees, but you'll have to wait until you hit Roanoke for the serious cliffs to appear.

At MP 31.5 you'll pass **Stillhouse Hollow Spring**, which was a legally operating distillery before Prohibition. Legend has it that the still manufactured 'moonshine' long after the 18th Amendment was passed, as did many other stills that operated in the mountains in the early 1900s. **Panther Mountain** is just ahead, named for the animals that once prowled the area. Though they've been extinct from here for quite some time, some people have reported a 'pantherlike' creature stalking the woods, creating a Bigfoot-style legend to terrify campers over a crackling campfire.

If you're a 'trainspotter,' don't miss the exhibit at the **Yankee Horse Ridge** parking area 2 miles ahead. A reconstructed narrow-gauge railway line is visible from the wooded overlook, and there's a small, 0.2-mile loop trail to the remote **Wigwam Falls**.

At **Indian Gap** (MP 47.5), you can't see anything but trees at first. You'll have to take the short trek to the true overlook. An easy, 0.3-mile trail begins in the parking area and loops past the SUV-size boulders at Indian Rocks. It's an excellent trail for young 'uns (supervised, of course), featuring an abundance of nooks and crannies and even a cave.

OTTER CREEK & JAMES RIVER

Map 2; MP 60.8

A major transportation hub during the Civil War, the James River contained a series of canal locks, which never really proved successful at taming the water. But it's the water today that lures travelers to the river banks, with creek fishing (there's a wheelchair-accessible fishing pier at Otter Creek, MP 63) and riverfront picnicking.

SIGHTS & ACTIVITIES

VISITOR CENTER (MP 63.6)

An exhibit on the restoration of one of the failed locks (Lock 7) is adjacent to the visitor center, which also includes restrooms, a restaurant and gift shop. Water is available onsite.

JAMES RIVER TRAIL

The easy, 0.4-mile trail features a footbridge that crosses under the Parkway bridge and leads to an exhibit on the Kanawha Canal Locks. It leaves from the visitor center parking lot.

TRAIL OF TREES

Also beginning at the parking lot is this moderate, 0.5-mile self-guided nature hike. You'll see a breathtaking view of the James River halfway into the walk.

SLEEPING & EATING

OTTER CREEK CAMPGROUND

☎ 434-299-5941; MP 61; campsite $14; ☯ year-round

Otter Creek is one of the loveliest campgrounds in the area, with many of its 45 first-come, first-served campsites perched alongside gurgling streams. Restrooms and water are available.

OTTER CREEK RESTAURANT

☎ 434-299-5862; ☯ May-Oct

This bona-fide log cabin in the woods serves what many travelers hail as the best buckwheat pancakes on the Parkway. Order a thick stack, then walk it off along the trickling creek. The menu includes sandwiches and heartier entrees for dinner.

ON THE ROAD

Located a few miles west of the Parkway, the **Cave Mountain Lake Recreation Area** (☎ 540-291-2188; entrance fee $5, campsite $15-20; ⏱ May-early Nov) is an isolated paradise with a 7-acre lake surrounded by hardwoods and pines. There's swimming and fishing from the sandy beach and shores, plus shaded lakefront picnic areas and a few easy-to-moderate hiking trails. Non-motorized boats are permitted in the lake. Hot showers are available at the bathhouse. From the Parkway, take US 501/VA 130 west (at MP 70, Petites Gap) and continue along US 130 at the split. About 3 miles later, make a left onto State Rd 759 and follow that 3 miles to State Rd 781. Turn right, and the lake is 1.6 miles further along.

Two trails leave from the Otter Creek area. The highlight of the strenuous, 3.4-mile (one way) **Apple Orchard Falls Trail** (MP 78.4) is a stunning 200ft waterfall. Look for the trailhead in the middle of the Sunset Fields Overlook parking lot. It starts immediately within the Jefferson National Forest and then passes over a section of the Appalachian Trail. A word of warning: This hike is classified as strenuous because of the 1000ft elevation change between the parking lot and the falls, so be prepared for steep climbs and descents.

The moderate, 1.6-mile **Fallingwater Cascades Trail Loop** (MP 83.1) also winds through a piece of the George Washington & Jefferson National Forest. It's a mild trek along a tumbling series of cascades that makes for a pleasant, quiet hike. Do this one in the fall for the sheer crush of color. It starts and ends at the Fallingwater Cascades Overlook; look for the stone staircase.

PEAKS OF OTTER

Maps 2 & 3; MP 85.9

A popular breather on the Parkway, Peaks of Otter is always packed with people. Rightly so, as the peaks form a striking triangle of mountains enclosing Abbott Lake: Sharp Top Mountain (3875ft), Flat Top Mountain (4001ft) and Harkening Hill (3372ft). Stone from Sharp Top was used in the building of the Washington Monument in Washington, DC.

You can also stop here for restrooms, picnic areas, a gas station, campground and water, and hikers and campers can stock up at the camp store. The **visitor center** contains a district ranger station, and the shuttle to Sharp Top Mountain departs from here.

SIGHTS & ACTIVITIES

POLLY WOOD'S ORDINARY

Ever been unhappy with your hotel room? Take a peek at the Ordinary, along the north shore of Abbott Lake, and see how lucky you really are. Polly Wood became a widow in 1830, and because she could not sustain herself by farming the small tract of land her husband willed to her, she opened her 'ordinary' home as an inn for travelers.

DETOUR: NATURAL BRIDGE

It's hardly the eighth wonder of the world, but **Natural Bridge** is a national historic landmark and one of the most spectacular sights of the Shenandoah Valley – a must-see for visitors to the region. The limestone arch, 215ft high and 90ft long, has been carved and shaped over the centuries by the seemingly lazy Cedar Creek, a tributary of the James River.

The Native American Monocan tribe worshipped the natural arch as the 'Bridge of God'; George Washington surveyed it for Lord Fairfax; Thomas Jefferson, impressed by its grandeur, purchased it at one stage; now, it supports a portion of VA 11.

Somehow, the beautiful, natural structure has been incorporated into a macabre complex known as the **Natural Bridge Inn & Conference Center** (☎ 800-533-1410, 540-291-2121; www.naturalbridgeva.com; ⏰ 8am–dark), which includes an attached wax museum, nearby caverns and an unspooky monster museum – the only truly frightening thing is the plethora of kitsch.

Your best bet, attraction-wise, is to take in the Natural Bridge from below (adult/child $10/5), the only real photographic angle. From June to September, the bridge is lit up after dark, but unfortunately you can't enjoy the experience without being subject to a preachy, over-the-top sound-and-light presentation called 'The Drama of Creation' (9pm and 10pm). Only the impressive sight of the arch at night justifies the high admission.

The most beautiful spot to camp near Natural Bridge is Cave Mountain Lake Recreation Area (see p18). But a fun alternative, especially for families, is **Yogi Bear's Jellystone Park Camp Resort at Natural Bridge** (☎ 800-258-9532; campsite/cabin $25/50 & up; 🖳), which features a lake with a swimming beach, tube rentals, a basketball court and a brand-new swimming pool. It's 5 miles from Natural Bridge; take exit 180A off VA 11 and go 3 miles on VA 130 east.

The **Colonial Dining Room** (⏰ Apr–Oct only) at Natural Bridge doles out rib-sticking Southern buffet grub on Friday and Saturday night. Also check out the Wednesday grill night and the gi-normous farm-fresh breakfasts buffets.

From the Parkway, take VA 501 west (just past the James River Visitor Center) to VA 130 south. You'll run right into VA 11 and Natural Bridge.

JOHNSON FARM

Johnson Farm dates back to the late 1700s, but it wasn't until 1852 that John T and Mary Elizabeth Johnson moved in and raised a whopping 13 children within these walls. Future families would raise even more kids here, all of whom collectively cared for the land by farming and gardening. Today it's an interpretive farmstead with living history demonstrations during warmer months, when visitors can help tend the garden, among other chores.

From the Peaks of Otter Visitor Center parking lot, an easy-to-moderate 2-mile trail parallels the lake at points and leads past both Polly Wood's Ordinary and Johnson Farm. It's also part of two other trails, Harkening Hill and Elk Run Loop.

SHARP TOP MOUNTAIN

One of the most commanding peaks in the Blue Ridge Mountains, Sharp Top is also one of the most recognized, thanks to its nearly perfect conical shape. It also marked the former northernmost boundary of the Cherokee Nation. Since the 19th century, it has been a favorite picnicking spot for locals, and it continues to grow in popularity – sometimes too much, particularly in summer. You can hike to the top, or forsake foot travel for the 10-minute ride on the modern **shuttle bus** ($4 one way), which departs from the Peaks of Otter Visitor Center.

The summit offers incredible views of the town of Bedford to the east; the James River Valley, Harkening Hill and the Alleghenies to the west; and the Parkway snaking north and south. The Peaks of Otter and Abbott Lake also appear as specks far below.

SHARP TOP TRAIL (MP 86)

A more difficult but rewarding way to reach the summit of Sharp Top is this strenuous, 1.5-mile trail. Begin at the camp store across the Parkway from the visitor center. The trail crosses the summit road (the shuttle-bus route) and makes a sharp switchback before coming to a junction with a trail leading to Buzzards Roost. Above the junction is the steepest part, with a staircase embedded in the hulking rocks. Suddenly the glorious summit appears above a rock garden of giant boulders, and you're guaranteed to encounter other people at this point.

On the summit you'll see a side path leading to the shuttle bus and a small shelter where you can hide away from bad weather or take a break for a quick snack. Either catch the bus here for the descent, or start back on the trail – walking on the summit road is prohibited.

SLEEPING & EATING

PEAKS OF OTTER CAMPGROUND

☎ 540-586-4357; MP 86; campsite $14; ☽ May-Oct

Ninety-two campsites lie in the shadow of Sharp Top Mountain, all available on a first-come, first-served basis. You'll find water, restrooms with flush toilets and cold-water sinks, but no shower facilities.

PEAKS OF OTTER LODGE

☎ 800-542-5927; www.peaksofotter.com; MP 86; r weekday/weekend $63/69 Nov 1-Apr 30, $86 May 1-Oct 31

The motel-style rooms are nothing fancy (and they're sans TV and phone), but they do command a fantastic view of Abbott Lake and Sharp Top Mountain.

PEAKS OF OTTER RESTAURANT

☎ 540-586-1081; ☽ breakfast, lunch & dinner year-round

There's not a bad seat in the house here, with floor-to-ceiling windows opening up onto a stunning view of the surrounding peaks and valleys. Fill up on 'Hikers' Delight Quiche' or some rich buttered apples before heading out on the trails.

ON THE ROAD

A sobering detour off the Parkway at VA 43 east (around MP 86) is the tiny town of Bedford, which, per capita, suffered the most casualties during WWII and hence was chosen to host an eerily moving tribute, the **National D-Day Memorial** (☎ 540-586-3329; www.dday. org; US 460 at US 122; $10/car; ☿ 10am-5pm). Among its towering arch and English flower garden, figures cast in bronze re-enact the 'storming of the beach,' complete with bursts of water symbolizing the hail of bullets the soldiers faced.

As you head south from Peaks of Otter, you'll pass through a series of 'Gaps' – none of which contain a rainbow of trendy clothing for sale. These gaps were passageways for Indians, settlers and even buffalo, the latter of which passed though **Powell's Gap** at MP 89.1. Farther ahead at MP 92.5, the **Sharp Top Overlook** offers an opportunity for a prime vacation photo of the mountain you might have just climbed. The Appalachian Trail, which parallels a good portion of this stretch down to Roanoke, crosses through the overlook's parking area.

A small cemetery dating from the 1900s appears a mile ahead at **Bobblet's Gap**, where seven members of the hardworking Bobblet family are buried. Keep an eye out for hawks and bald eagles on the approach to **Harvey's Knob Overlook** (MP 95.3), especially during migration season in September. For the next 4 miles, you'll encounter references to the area's iron-mining history, which boomed during the Civil War and the early 1900s. This includes the **Great Valley Overlook** (MP 99.6), where you can peer down into a current dolomite quarry (the mineral used to pave roads and highways).

ROANOKE MOUNTAIN

Map 3; MP 120.3

A quick, 10-minute jaunt on the **Roanoke Mountain Summit Trail** leads to a dramatic view of Roanoke and Mill Mountain. Farther north, at MP 114, is the **Roanoke River Trail**, which affords stunning views of the river and the Niagara Hydroelectric dam. This overlook is another of the Parkway's launch sites for hang-gliding.

The fairly secluded **Roanoke Mountain Campground** (☎ 540-767-2492; campsite $14; ☿ May-Oct) makes for a good night's sleep before you explore the Roanoke area. The first-come, first-served facilities include 74 campsites, water, restrooms and cold-water faucets, but no showers. There's a pay phone at the registration hut.

ROANOKE

Population 95,000; Map 8

Illuminated by its giant star, Roanoke is the big city in these parts, with a compact set of attractions based around a great downtown farmers market. As the Parkway curves east 'round the city, the landscape changes dramatically, as if a giant hand squashed the mountain peaks flat into gently rolling farmland. As soon as you pass Roanoke Mountain, you'll reach the junction with US 220. Head west on US 220 for about 2 miles and you'll run smack into the city. Three other roads off the Parkway will take you into Roanoke as well: US 460 at MP 105.6, VA 24 at MP 112, and Mill Mountain Spur Rd at MP 121.5.

SIGHTS & ACTIVITIES

CENTER IN THE SQUARE
☎ 540-342-5700; www.centerinthesquare.org; 1 Market Square; ☽ 10am-5pm Tue-Sat, 1-5pm Sun
This is the hub of activity in downtown Roanoke, with a science museum, theater, planetarium, local history museum and free art museum showcasing the work of folk and local artists.

MILL MOUNTAIN
There are several attractions atop this picturesque mountaintop. **Mill Mountain Zoo** (☎ 540-343-3241; www.mmzoo.org; adult/child 3-12 $6.75/4.50; ☽ 10am-4:30pm) and an adjacent wildflower garden, both perched on a hilltop near the Parkway, are perfect for the kids – the 'zoo choo' is $2 extra. Directly next door are the **Roanoke Star** and a breathtaking view of the city. **Virginia's Explore Park** (☎ 800-842-9163, 540-427-1800; www.explorepark.org; adult/child 3-11 $8/4.50; ☽ 10am-5pm Wed-Sat, from noon Sun Apr-Oct) uses living history demonstrations to capture three centuries of the area's past.

To get to Mill Mountain from downtown Roanoke, take Jefferson St south to Walnut. Turn left on Walnut, cross over a bridge and continue straight up the mountain. From the Parkway, look for signs for Roanoke Mountain Campground and Mill Mountain (at approximately MP 120.4) and take the spur road up the mountain.

VIRGINIA MUSEUM OF TRANSPORTATION
☎ 540-342-5670; www.vmt.org; 303 Norfolk Ave SW; adult/child 3-11 $7.40/5.25; ☽ 11am-4pm Mon-Fri, 10am-5pm Sat, from 1pm Sun
The hands-on exhibits, especially the locomotive garden in which you can walk through creaky, old train cars, will thrill kids and trains-potters alike.

HARRISON MUSEUM OF AFRICAN AMERICAN CULTURE
☎ 540-345-4818; 523 Harrison Ave; admission free; ☽ 1-5pm Tue-Sun
An intimate museum chronicles the impact of black Americans on the history of the area.

ROANOKE VALLEY CONVENTION & VISITORS BUREAU
☎ 540-342-6025; www.visitroanokeva.com; 101 Shenandoah Ave NE; ☽ 9am-5pm
Stop by the old Norfolk and Western railway station for maps and local information. You can also find out about hikes run by the Roanoke Appalachian Trail Club and rides organized by the Blue Ridge Bicycle Club.

SLEEPING & EATING

HOTEL ROANOKE & CONFERENCE CENTER
☎ 540-985-5900; www.hotelroanoke.com; 110 Shenandoah Ave NE; r from $84

This grand belle of the South has faithfully integrated 1882 features into an ultramodern hotel, with modern luxuries such as high-speed Internet access in every rose-tinted guest room. The swimming pools and proximity to area attractions make it a good base for families.

PATRICK HENRY HOTEL
☎ 540-345-8811, 800-303-0988; 617 S Jefferson St; r from $70

Though no fries come with these 'supersize' hotel rooms, kitchenettes, complimentary airport shuttles, a public laundry room and free health-club facilities do. This surprisingly affordable, renovated downtown hotel is just 3 blocks from Center in the Square.

HISTORIC ROANOKE CITY MARKET
☎ 540-342-2028; 213 Market St; ☻ 7:30am-5pm Mon-Sat

The farmers market dates from 1882, when it was a meager assortment of 25 stands. Today it's the oldest continuously operating farmers market in Virginia and holds a bounty of fresh, modern foods to eat in or take away. There's also an eclectic assortment of craft stands selling everything from hummingbird feeders to fused glass to hand-painted metal garden ornaments.

PARADOX
☎ 540-343-6644; 202 Market Square; dishes $7-20; ☻ dinner

Living up to its name, this restaurant–music venue mixes international tastes (Greek pizza, pork *cubano* and chicken *provençal*) with what can only be described as bizarre live acts ranging from kung-fu karaoke and vaudeville to funk and soul. It's a must for sheer atmosphere, and there are killer martinis to boot.

TEXAS TAVERN
☎ 540-342-4825; 114 W Church Ave

A beloved hole-in-the-wall staple for lunching locals, the tavern is tiny, so nab a seat if you can and enjoy the fiery chili bowls ($3).

AROUND ROANOKE

Map 3

From Roanoke, take US 220 east to return to the Parkway. Alternatively, you can take US 116 east from Roanoke to Burnt Chimney, then US 122 north to the following attractions.

Twenty miles east of Roanoke, the **Booker T Washington National Monument** (☎ 540-721-2094; US 122; admission free; ☻ 9am-5pm) is a re-created tobacco farm honoring the former slave who became an international African American leader and educator.

Smith Mountain Lake is Virginia's second-largest body of water. The **Smith Mountain Lake State Park** (☎ 540-297-6066; www.dcr. state.va.us/parks/smithmtn.htm; 1235 State Park Rd) comes alive in summer, with a plethora of biking, hiking and fishing options, as well as cool waterfront **cabins** (☎ 800-933-PARK; from $68). It's 25 miles southeast of Roanoke, on US 122.

ON THE ROAD

Return to the Parkway from US 116 and continue south; here the landscape really starts to open up.

What could you get for $15 in 1877? A tract of land, believe it or not. And that's what the local government paid the Kelley family to build a one-room schoolhouse. The **Kelley Schoolhouse** (MP 147) is the only remaining schoolhouse building on the Parkway.

The name **Smart View** (MP 154.5) comes from the beautiful vistas of the mountains and valleys ahead. You'll find a small recreation area with an exhibit on the Trail Cabin; pioneers lived in this one-room cabin and sustained themselves on the surrounding land and the single freshwater spring. Today there are restrooms and picnic areas, as well as a few leg-stretcher trails.

At **Tuggle Gap** (MP 165.3), take VA 8 west and prepare for an extremely twisty ride down from the Parkway straight into **Floyd County**. This southeastern region of Virginia is synonymous with bluegrass, and the tiny town of **Floyd** is the mecca of mountain music.

You haven't experienced bluegrass until you visit the legendary **Floyd Country Store** (☎ 540-745-4563; www.floydcountrystore.com; 206 S Locust St). The **Friday Night Jamborees** (adult/child 16 & under $3/free; ☻ performances 6:30-11:30pm) draw record crowds – it's not unusual to see children clogging to frenetic banjo twangs alongside a blue-haired betty cutting a rug with a visiting city slicker. Saturdays feature more great music from local and national bands ($15), and in summer, musicians often spill into alleys, driveways and parking lots, making for a giant jam session.

Not far from the store is another music venue, the **Jacksonville Center** (☎ 540-745-2784), where performances and festivals take place inside a refurbished old barn.

ROCKY KNOB AREA

Maps 3 & 4; MP 167

SIGHTS

ROCKY KNOB VISITOR CENTER (MP 169)

The small **visitor center** has a pay phone, restrooms and a picnic area with a shelter. You'll find two leg-stretcher trails from the picnic area: the 1-mile **Rocky Knob Picnic Area Loop Trail** and the 3.1-mile **Black Ridge Trail**. The Loop Trail is a gentle trail circling the picnic area through hemlock and thickets of rhododenron.

MABRY MILL (MP 176.2)

Built in 1910, this historic water-powered grist mill is now the most photographed spot on the Parkway. The cabins feature National Park Service demonstrations of blacksmithing, carving, weaving and other jobs of early pioneer life.

MEADOWS OF DAN (MP 177)

This farming community (its name comes from the Old Testament) was a bustling epicenter of Appalachian life in the early 1900s. Mabry Mill served as a gathering place for the town, providing work as well as a social release from the labor-intensive lives these settlers endured.

SLEEPING & EATING

ROCKY KNOB CAMPGROUND
☎ 540-745-9660; MP 167; campsite $14; ⊙ May-Oct
At this quiet campground you can imagine what early settlers at Mabry Mill came home to at night. There are 81 campsites available on a first-come, first-served basis.

MEADOWS OF DAN CAMPGROUND
☎ 276-952-2292; 2182 Jeb Stuart Hwy, MP 177.7; campsite/cabin $18/79-165
This privately owned campground makes a good base for exploring Mabry Mill and the Floyd area. Just off the Parkway at US 58 west, it boasts coveted showers, washers and dryers. Cozy cabins come outfitted with TVs, VCRs, refrigerators and microwaves – roughing it never felt so good. Open year-round.

Wine in the Woods

Parkway wildflowers are beautiful in spring, but sniff another type of mountain bouquet at two hidden wineries.

Chateau Morrisette (☎ 540-593-2865; MP 171.5; www.chateaumorrisette.com; ⊙ 10am-5pm Mon-Thu, until 6pm Fri & Sat, from 11am Sun) is a rustic winery with a sprawling grand hall, two loveable black Labs and a yummy restaurant onsite. And hey, forget the designated driver – you can reach this winery on foot! Start at the Rocky Knob Visitor Center (MP 169) and head along the loop trail until you hit the Blue Blaze Trail. Take the Blue Blaze Trail across the Parkway and then onto a gravel road. Make a right onto a secondary road running alongside the Parkway. Then cross the Parkway again and head for a stand of trees on your left. After walking through, turn left at the intersection and make a right onto 'Winery Road,' which leads a mile to the winery.

Neighboring **Villa Appalaccia** (☎ 540-593-3100; MP 170; www.villaappalaccia.com; 752 Rock Castle Gorge; ⊙ 11am-5pm Thu & Fri, 11am-6pm Sat, noon-4pm Sun) is an equally stately winery that embodies the style of an Italian country home. Play a game of bocce ball while sampling a Pinot Grigio or listen to live folk music in the garden on Saturday night. To get here, immediately after the MP 170 sign, make a left onto VA 720 and follow the gravel driveway to the winery.

ROCKY KNOB CABINS

☎ 276-952-2947; MP 174; cabin $57, extra person $8, rollaway bed $8, firewood $3.50; ☺ late May-Oct 31

You'll find just a refrigerator, kitchenette and linens in these rustic yet cozy cabins close to popular Mabry Mill. A bathhouse and comfort station are only a short, flashlight-guided trek away. There's a discount if you stay multiple nights.

MABRY MILL RESTAURANT

☎ 276-952-2947; MP 176; dishes $4-15; ☺ seasonal

The small restaurant adjacent to the mill's gift shop serves the best buckwheat pancakes this side of the Appalachian Trail. You can also order a basic lunch or dinner, but get there early to beat the tour bus entourages.

ON THE ROAD

Back on the Parkway, **Groundhog Mountain** (MP 188.8) is a well-shaded turnout with restrooms and picnic tables. Here you'll find displays of the three basic fence forms found along the Parkway: snake, post and rail, and buck. Strangely, a small cemetery occu-

---

DETOUR: MOUNT AIRY

Well golllly! The inspiration for the fictional town Mayberry from *The Andy Griffith Show*, Mount Airy was the star's hometown – and they sure don't let you forget it. You can get your picture snapped in front of the Barney Fife squad car outside the police department, your hair cut in Floyd's City Barber Shop, your pork chop sandwich prepared at the Snappy Lunch counter, then fall asleep in Aunt Bee's Room at the Mayberry Motor Inn.

If you're not big into Mayberry lore, check out the bizarrely fascinating story of the most famous conjoined twins, Eng and Chang, who were buried just outside town. After grueling hours touring with PT Barnum's circus and exhaustive medical examinations, they decided to retire near Mount Airy, where they adopted the last name of 'Bunker,' married a pair of sisters and had 21 children between them. On a return trip from Europe, Chang suffered a stroke and later contracted a fatal case of bronchitis. It's said that Eng died shortly after from pure shock upon realizing his brother had died. The **visitor center** (☎ 800-576-0231, 336-789-4636; 615 N Main St; ☺ 9am-5pm Mon-Sat, 11am-4:30pm Sun) and **Mount Airy Museum of Regional History** (☎ 336-786-4478; www.northcarolinamuseum.org; 301 N Main St; ☺ 10am-4pm Tue-Fri, until 2pm Sat) feature exhibits on Eng and Chang's life and can give you directions to the grave site.

Even stranger, this pokey town is a tech-savvy WiFi hub – you can check your e-mail by popping your computer open anywhere downtown!

From the Parkway, Mount Airy is a straight shot east on US 52.

---

pies an island in the parking lot. From the lot, a quick trail leads to an observation tower with a good view of Groundhog.

Further ahead is the **Puckett Cabin parking area** (MP 190), named for Orlena Puckett, a midwife who delivered more than 1000 babies in her Civil War–era career, charging a mere $6 for her services. Ironically, none of her own 24 children lived past the age of two.

One of the most anticipated attractions on the Parkway, the new **Blue Ridge Music Center** (MP213; ☎ 276-236-5309; www.blueridgemusiccenter.net) is a collaboration between the NPS and the National Council for the Traditional Arts. It will be a major educational resource devoted to preserving and promoting the roots of local mountain music. As of this writing, only the amphitheater is open to host the center's summer concert series on weekends. Most concerts are free, but tickets to big-name bands start at $10. The center eventually plans to feature film screenings, a listening library, a museum and a system of trails designed to showcase the evolution of this old-timey art form.

SLEEPING & EATING

MISTY ROSE COTTAGE
☎ 276-236-7658; www.pdbloghomes.com; MP 202-203; r $120
This cozy two-bedroom home is just a pebble's throw from the Parkway. It features a fully stocked kitchenette, a small hot tub on the screened-in back porch and comfy rocking chairs on the front porch, providing a perfect setting for a mountain sunset.

HI BLUE RIDGE MOUNTAINS
☎ 276-236-4962; MP 214.5; dm $17; ☒ closed Jan; no credit cards
Once you reach MP 214, look for a gray iron pipe gate that marks the hidden entrance to this popular mountain hostel. Enjoy fantastic views and a toe-tapping music room. Guests are encouraged to bring musical instruments.

MOUNTAIN VIEW RESTAURANT
☎ 276-728-9196; MP 199; meals from $3
Down-home breakfast platters piled high with hash browns and grits draw plenty of repeat business. And they're a bargain – all are less than $10. It's just off the Parkway at the junction of US 52 in Fancy Gap.

GALAX

Population 6900; Map 4
On the cusp of Virginia and North Carolina, Galax is a classic slice of hometown America in the mountains. Dubbed the 'world's capital of bluegrass music,' it lives up to that nickname by hosting a slew of concerts throughout the year. In early August, the **Old Fiddler's Convention** (☎ 276-236-8541; www.oldfiddlersconvention.com; nightly/season ticket $5-10/30), Galax's biggest hootenanny, draws the best fiddlers in the country to jam with fellow dulcimer,

banjo, mouth-harp and bull-fiddle players (think Woodstock with a major twang).

Get there one of two ways: at MP 199.8, take US 52 west toward Hillsville, then US 58/221 south; or, for a more scenic route, at MP 205.5 take VA 97 south directly into Galax.

SIGHTS & ACTIVITIES

REX THEATRE
☎ 276-238-8130; www.rextheatergalax.org; E Grayson St; admission by donation; ☺ 8-10pm
On Friday nights, this is the place to be for the live radio broadcast of traditional bluegrass music on the 'Blue Ridge Backroads' show, one of only three live bluegrass old-time radio shows in the country. If you can't make it to the theater, tune in on 98.1FM.

GALAX TOURISM OFFICE
☎ 276-238-8130; www.ingalax.net; 111 E Grayson St
For more sights, activities and events in Galax, call these folks or visit the helpful website. Also check www.visitgalax.com, which was still under construction at press time.

SLEEPING & EATING

SUPER 8 MOTEL
☎ 276-236-5127, 800-800-8000; 303 N Main St; d from $49
There's not a lot of choice for sleeping in Galax, but then again, there aren't many motels with a retired mechanical bull fronting their lobbies. Rooms are big and clean, and the motel is centrally located within walking distance to restaurants and the Rex Theatre.

THE SMOKEHOUSE
☎ 276-236-1000; 101 N Main St; dishes under $10
A colorful hangout with award-winning barbecue – most people chow here before heading to the Rex Theatre across the street.

MACADO'S
☎ 276-236-0399; 201 N Main St; dishes under $15
For a grab-and-go meal, try the giant, stuffed deli sandwiches.

SOUTHWEST VIRGINIA FARMER'S MARKET
☎ 276-728-5540; US 58 at I-77 and N Main St; ☺ Jun 1–mid-Oct
Get up early on Friday and Saturday mornings to get the best pick of fresh fruits, homemade pastries and gorgeous flower bundles.

NORTH CAROLINA

The Parkway stretches for 262 glorious miles in North Carolina, where the meadows give way to alpine vistas. Between the towering peaks, the North Carolina section can lay claim to impressive manmade structures around Grandfather Mountain, an assortment of talented craftspeople and their workshops, the beautiful arches of its 26 tunnels, and Asheville, a gem of a city with a lot of Southern charm.

CUMBERLAND KNOB

Map 4; MP 217.5

This is where it all started, on September 11, 1935. The groundbreaking of the Parkway began at Cumberland Knob, and the information center is one of the earliest structures still standing.

Pick up Parkway maps, books and a small assortment of gifts at the **visitor center** (☎ 336-657-8161). Along with restrooms and a spacious picnic area, you'll find an old cemetery that reveals how short and hard life was in the mountains. A young mother, Rebecca Moxley, had asked to be buried under an apple tree, as she feared she wouldn't live much past the birth of her son. As predicted, she did indeed pass away after her son's birth and now rests here, among other family members.

Two trails depart from here: the easy, half-mile **Cumberland Knob Trail** and the strenuous, 2-mile **Gully Creek Trail**. The Cumberland loop is nothing spectacular, just a lazy-day hike up to a historic stone structure that's unfortunately succumbed to 21st-century graffiti. However, the Gully Creek Trail skirts a refreshing mountain stream and makes for a rewarding hike.

There are some good roadside observation points to the south. At MP 232.5, pull into the **Stone Mountain Overlook** to examine the 500ft granite patch opposite, which looks like a bump on the head. It's a heavenly spot for a picnic, too. Three miles on, the **Devil's Garden** is the gap formed by two crags; rattlesnakes and copperheads have made their home there.

DOUGHTON PARK

Map 4; MP 239–248

This meadowed landscape was originally called 'The Bluffs', but it was renamed in honor of Congressman Robert L Doughton, who was an avid supporter of the Parkway. Today it's known for its abundant wildlife – you might spy red and gray foxes, white-tailed deer and the occasional bobcat.

Within the park are several lodging options, including Bluffs Lodge and a campground, and it's one of the areas where backcountry camping is allowed on the Parkway.

Pick up maps and fuel up at the **Bluffs gas station** (MP 241).

The White Stuff

The Parkway is a favorite warm-weather journey, but don't overlook the wintry season. Crowds are blessedly sparse, and there are plenty of activities that allow you to enjoy the snowy backdrop.

- **Wintergreen Resort** (☎ 434-325-2100; all-day lift ticket midweek adult/child 6-12/child under 6 $40/33/free, ski rentals $32/27/22, snowboarding $42/37/NA; tubing midweek/weekend $18/22; ☼ Oct-Mar) is the oldest ski resort in the state. Of the 23 trails, about 20% are beginner, 42% intermediate, 21% advanced and 17% expert. A 1003ft vertical drop is served by double, triple, quad and two six-person high-speed chairlifts. For family fun, or to satisfy that kid inside, hit the two tubing runs: the 10-lane monster hill, **The Plunge** (ages 6 and older), and **The Slide** (ages 2 and older). Snowboarders can catch some serious air in the terrain park, which features fun boxes and rainbow and battleship rails. (For directions, see p13.)

- **Massanutten Resort** (☎ 800-207-6277; www.massresort.com; all-day lift ticket midweek adult/child 6-12/child under 6 $35/30/free, ski rentals $20/16/16, snowboarding $42/37/NA; ☼ 9am-10pm Dec–mid-Mar), north of Waynesboro, boasts a vertical drop of 1110ft (the highest in Virginia) and 14 slopes (including the 3400ft Diamond Jim and 4100ft ParaDice), all of which are lit at night. There is one quad chairlift, and the field has 100% snow-making capacity. A lot of ski racing happens here, and the resort includes a PSIA ski school and SKIwee program. The mid-Atlantic snowboard series takes place in early February. The tubing park is extremely popular and usually sells out – call a day in advance ($16 for two hours). To get there, take US 340 north from Waynesboro and turn left on VA 649. After 2 miles, turn right on VA 33 and go 1 mile to VA 644; the entrance is on the right.

- **Appalachian Ski Mountain** (☎ 800-322-2373, 828-295-7828; www.appskimtn.com; all-day lift ticket midweek adult/child 6-12/child under 6 $26/18/free, ski rentals $12/9/9, snowboarding $22; ☼ mid-Dec–mid-Mar) is the most family-oriented range around, with nine gentle downhills, snowboarding and an ice-skating rink. It's on US 221/331 between Boone and Blowing Rock.

- **Ski Beech** (☎ 800-438-2093, 828-387-2011; www.skibeech.com; 1007 Beech Mountain Pkwy; all-day lift ticket midweek adult/child 5-12/child under 5 $28/21/free, ski rentals $19, snowboarding $25; ☼ late Nov–mid-March), not far from Boone in Beech Mountain, towers 5506ft above sea level and boasts an excellent outdoor ice-skating rink ($12 including rentals). From Boone, take NC 105 south to NC 184 west and follow the signs.

- **Sugar Mountain** (☎ 800-784-2768; www.skisugar.com; all-day lift ticket midweek adult/child 5-11/child under 5 $26/21/free; ski rentals $12/8/8; snowboarding $22; tubing weekday/weekend $15/20; ☼ Oct-Mar), about 15 minutes from Boone, is one of the few southeastern ski resorts to break a 1000ft vertical slope. From Boone, take NC 105 south to NC 184 west and follow the signs.

SIGHTS & ACTIVITIES

BRINEGAR CABIN (MP 238.5)
The former home of local farmer Martin Brinegar, this wood cabin offers a glimpse into daily life in the early 1900s. Adjacent to the cabin is a vegetable garden tended by the park service. Living history demonstrations, including weaving on the old loom, take place in summer. Trailheads for the strenuous, 4.2-mile Cedar Ridge Trail and moderate, 7.5-mile Bluff Mountain Trail are in the parking lot.

BLUFF MOUNTAIN TRAIL (MP 244.7)
This trail parallels the Parkway. With only moderate elevation changes, it's an excellent walk for beginners. Pack a picnic to enjoy at the shelter near the end of the path. Start at the Alligator Back Overlook in Doughton Park – the views from the overlook alone should pump you up for the hike to the peak of Bluff Mountain. Take the stone steps to the bottom and make a left onto the trail. You'll soon encounter a series of switchbacks, and the climb turns steep, first passing through dense forest, then spilling out onto bald cliffs. Cove Creek Basin is visible on clear days.

Go through two fences, the first just before the trail turns right at the red blaze, and the second on the way toward the mountaintop, where you'll find that open shelter. If you packed your lunch, linger a little here, admiring the craggy peaks in the distance. Pack up and continue along the ridgeline until ending at the Brinegar Cabin, where you can explore this old farmstead and perhaps drop in on a living-history demonstration.

SLEEPING & EATING

DOUGHTON PARK CAMPGROUND
☎ 336-372-8568; MP 241.1; campsite $14; ☼ May-Oct
This campground is popular with families, perhaps because of its close proximity to interpretive sites like the Brinegar Cabin, as well as easy hiking trails. There are 110 shaded campsites, and guests might hear occasional traffic noise coming from the Parkway. Amenities include a gas station, restrooms, flush toilets and water, trails, nearby food services and a campfire circle for evening programs.

RACCOON HOLLER
☎ 336-982-2706; 493 Raccoon Holler Rd, MP 259; campsite $17
This quaint lakeside campground offers fishing, showers, laundry and a small camp store. Make a right off the Parkway at MP 259.

BLUFFS LODGE
☎ 336-372-4499; www.blueridgeresort.com; MP 241.1; s/d $79, extra person $8, rollaway bed $8; ☼ late May-Oct 31
There's a great open-air fireplace on the stone verandah, but otherwise it's no frills in these small, motel-style rooms with no TVs or phones.

It's Beginning to Look a Lot Like Christmas

You can't throw a pine cone in northwest North Carolina without hitting a Christmas tree farm. Fraser firs, white pine, Colorado blue spruce, Leyland cypress and red cedar trees blanket hundreds of acres of hilly landscapes – it's a sight worthy of any Norman Rockwell painting. North Carolina produces approximately 50 million Carolina Fraser firs, ranking the state second in Christmas-tree production – that's a heck of a lot of presents.

Around Thanksgiving, crowds swoop in to chop, bag and carry out the perfect Christmas tree, many of them making mini-vacations out of the ceremonious cutting. Contact the **North Carolina Christmas Tree Association** (☎ 800-562-8789, 828-262-5826; www.ncchristmastrees.com) for more information.

Make your own holiday memories with an overnight stay at the **River House Inn** (☎ 336-982-2109; www.riverhousenc.com; 1896 Old Field Creek Rd, Grassy Creek; d $115-150), a delightful gem hidden off the Parkway, nestled at the end of a rocky drive and overlooking the gentle New River. The main house boasts comfy porch rockers, an intimate bar and an award-winning restaurant. Guest rooms are scattered throughout quaint cottages, each with a cozy gas fireplace and huge Jacuzzi tub (but no TVs, phones or keys!). The friendly staff make you feel like one of the gang – have a chat with owner Gail Winston about her incredible life story.

From MP 228 on the Parkway, take US 21 west to VA 93 south. From there, go south on VA 16 toward Grassy Creek, and look for the signs.

BLUFFS COFFEE SHOP
☎ 336-372-4744; MP 241.1; dishes $5-15; 🕒 7:30am-7:30pm May-Nov

The buckwheat pancakes with cooked apples are legendary here. It's a convenient meeting spot for coffee and a quick bite.

BLUFFS RESTAURANT
☎ 336-372-4499; MP241.1; dishes $5-12; 🕒 May-Nov

Just across the Parkway is this slightly more expensive option, offering rib-sticking country fare like stuffed ham and corn dishes served up a million different ways.

ON THE ROAD

A spacious gift shop, the **Northwest Trading Post** (☎ 336-982-2543; MP 259; 🕒 9am-5:30pm Apr 1-Oct 31) sells homemade crafts from local artisans. All gifts marked with white tags are certified by the NPS as authentic Indian craftsmanship.

Beginning at the **Jumpinoff Rock** parking area (MP 260.3), the easy, 0.5-mile **Jumpinoff Rock Trail** skirts the valley and ends with a spectacular view atop 'sheer rock cliffs.

There's a 30-minute leisurely hiking loop (0.6 miles) from **Cascades Overlook** (MP 271.0) winding down through a hemlock forest to a spectacular 'cascading' waterfall.

Another trail (0.5 miles) leads to the **Cool Springs Baptist Church** and the **Jesse Brown Cabin** buildings. You'll also find restrooms and a shaded picnic area, with plenty of room for impromptu bluegrass performances – you might just see one if you stop.

Taking up a 2-mile stretch of the Parkway, **EB Jeffress Park** (MP 272) features an overlook with a trail leading to a steep waterfall. It's named after EB Jeffress, a strong supporter of the Blue Ridge Parkway project who fought against making it a toll road. He was also the chairman of the North Carolina State Highway and Public Works Commission in 1933.

At MP 285.1, you'll come to **Daniel Boone's Trace**. This tiny parking area sports a bronze plaque and a historical marker at the spot where, local legend has it, Daniel Boone passed through on his way to Kentucky.

BOONE

Population 13,500; Map 5
Named the 'firefly capital of America,' this artists' colony on US 221/421 boasts an electrifying assortment of outdoor activities as well as a few kitschy attractions and even an old-fashioned drugstore counter. Pick up information at the **Convention & Visitors Bureau** (☎ 800-852-9506; www.visitboonenc.com; 208 Howard St). To get to Boone, exit the Parkway at about MP 292, taking US 321 north (US 321 south takes you to Blowing Rock).

SIGHTS & ACTIVITIES

WAHOO'S WHITEWATER RAFTING AND CANOE OUTFITTERS
☎ 800-444-RAFT; www.wahoosadventures.com; US 321S; ⏱ year-round
Ever been white-water canoeing? Wahoo's can help you do it, along with lazy tubing, traditional canoeing (plus picnic lunches), swimming and braving Class V rapids.

THE HORN IN THE WEST
☎ 828-264-2120; admission $15; ⏱ late Jun–mid-Aug
This musical drama attempts to 'relive the frontier days with Daniel Boone' at an amphitheater off Blowing Rock Rd.

EATING

MURPHY'S RESTAURANT & PUB
☎ 828-264-5117; 747 W King St; ⏱ restaurant 11am-10pm, bar 11am- 2am
Try Murphy's for great beer specials, big burgers and burritos for $5 to $7.

ANGELICA'S
☎ 828-265-0809; 506 W King St; ⏱ 11am-10pm Mon-Sat
Angelica's is a New Age veggie joint with a juice bar. Who would have reckoned on toasted seaweed sheets ($5 to $8) up here?

ON THE ROAD

If you're in the area, be sure to pay a visit to the **Mast General Store** (☎ 828-963-6511), on NC 194 in Valle Crucis (about 30 minutes' drive west of Boone). A quaint, old-fashioned place with a potbelly stove, it's just this side of contrived but stacked to the gills with everything from thick woolen socks to gout cures. Here you can pick up mountain toys such as the 'gee-haw whimmy diddle,' a stick with a propeller that turns when you rub the notches on the stick.

Tweetsie Railroad (☎ 800-526-5740, 828-264-9061; www.tweetsie.com; adult/child 3-12 $25/18; ⊙ 9am-6pm daily late May–mid-Aug, 9am-6pm Fri-Sun late Aug-late Oct & late Apr-late May), in between Boone and Blowing Rock, is a great, if somewhat hokey, family-oriented theme park. Wee cowpokes get a taste of the Wild West by helping the US Marshall fend off train robbers, sampling down-home grub and experiencing country fair rides and music. There are even a few 'modern' arcade games to keep the tiny ones happy. From the Parkway, take the Boone exit at MP 291 and follow the signs (just listen for the 'tweet tweet' as you approach the park).

BLOWING ROCK

Population 1500; Map 5

Reminiscent of a quaint New England coastal town (without the ocean!), Blowing Rock is just a mile off the Parkway on US 321 south. Main St is a tightly packed, colorful corridor with flowery B&Bs, shops and open-air restaurants. The town makes for a charming sleepover, especially at the exciting Chetola Resort.

SIGHTS & ACTIVITIES

The Blowing Rock and Mystery Hill are basically tourist traps and not necessarily worth the high admission prices. Neither attraction manages to impress adults (unless your last name is 'Griswold'), but hey, if it's a rainy day, the kids might think they're cool.

THE BLOWING ROCK

☎ 828-295-7111; www.theblowingrock.com; adult/child 4-11 $6/4; ⊙ daily Mar-Dec, weekends Jan & Feb

The Blowing Rock is a lot of hot wind about an Indian legend and a lovers' leap. You'll get the whole story on the tour, but basically it's a cliff with an unusual wind pattern that blows objects back at you. It's just outside the town's center, south on US 321.

MYSTERY HILL

☎ 828-264-2792; 129 Mystery Hill Lane; www.mysteryhill-nc.com; adult/senior/child 5 & up $8/6/5; ⊙ 8am-8pm Jun-Aug, 9am-5pm Sep-May

Several museums make up this complex, but the biggest oddball attraction is Mystery House. The slightly rundown home claims to harbor a strange energy pattern that exerts a stronger pull of gravity and that defies the laws of physics. Balls and water move uphill, and wallets are inexplicably emptied...

APPALACHIAN CULTURAL MUSEUM
☎ 828-262-3117; University Hall Dr off Blowing Rock Rd; adult/child 10-18/senior $4/2/3.50; ⏲ 10am-5pm Tue-Sat, 1-5pm Sun

A serious attempt to present mountain life and history beyond the hillbilly stereotypes, this museum in the Mystery Hill complex features some first-class exhibits and thoughtful interpretive material.

BLOWING ROCK CHAMBER OF COMMERCE
☎ 800-295-7851; www.blowingrock.com; 132 Park St

The visitor center is perfectly located between Chetola and downtown. Come here for maps, brochures and accommodations info.

BLOWING ROCK EQUESTRIAN CENTER
☎ 828-295-4700; 1500 Laurel Ave off NC 221; 1hr/2hr $35/50; ⏲ 9am, 11am, 1pm, 3pm, 5pm & 6:30pm

Adults and children older than 9 can enjoy leisurely trail rides through hemlock forest and up to Flat Top Manor (p36).

HIGH MOUNTAIN EXPEDITIONS
☎ 800-262-9036; www.highmountainexpeditions.com; Main St; ⏲ year-round

Less than 2 miles from the Parkway, this adventure company offers a little bit of everything, from rides on frothy rapids (starting at $49/44 adult/child) to spelunking ($75 per person) to kayak rentals ($15 for four hours). For some expeditions, you must have a minimum of four people.

SLEEPING & EATING

CHETOLA RESORT
☎ 800-CHETOLA; www.chetola.com; N Main St; r/condo $86-106/130-140 Jan-Apr, $131-141/170-195 May-Dec

Don't let the term 'resort' deter you from missing this beautiful, affordable complex just 1 mile off the Parkway. Individual condos create a home-away-from-home atmosphere, and you'll be spoiled at the spa. It's a great place for families, with an indoor swimming pool, playground and sparkling lake where kids can hike or chase the geese. From here you can walk to downtown Blowing Rock.

SIX PENCE PUB
☎ 828-295-3155; 1121 Main St; dishes $6-23; ⏲ 11:30am-2am

A touch of the Old Country on Main Street, USA. Guinness and fish and chips are the specialties, but you can't go wrong with the over-stuffed pot pies.

CHEESEBURGER GRILL & PARADISE BAR
☎ 828-295-4858; US 221 at Main St; dishes $7-19

The signature massive burgers and spicy wings fire up hikers and Harley riders alike after a long day on the Parkway.

KILWIN'S
☎ 828-295-3088; 1087 Main St; scoops from $3.50
Save room for a Blowing Rock specialty – a scoop of rich homemade ice cream at this wildly popular scoop shop, and savor your cone on one of the park benches across the street.

MOSES H CONE MEMORIAL PARK
Map 5; MP 294
A 2-mile stretch of the Parkway, this park takes its name from Moses Cone, the so-called 'Blue Denim King' who owned a pants factory in Greensboro. The park includes his former home, the breathtaking Flat Top Manor, a not-so-ordinary crafts shop and 25 miles of carriage trails that start from the visitor center parking lot and wind among wild thickets of blueberries, wildflower meadows and hemlock forest.

SIGHTS & ACTIVITIES

VISITOR CENTER
The center, housed just inside Flat Top Manor, boasts a comprehensive selection of reading material on the region, including cookbooks, bicycle-trail descriptions, flora and fauna handbooks, and even ghost stories. The center also offers Junior Ranger programs for kids on Sunday and free evening entertainment on Friday and Saturday, including a moonlight tour of the Cone graves, which lie about a mile away. Restrooms are only a short walk from the center, but be forewarned that they close at 8pm (6pm Nov-Apr).

Horseback riding is popular along the Cone trails; see Blowing Rock Equestrian Center (p35).

FLAT TOP MANOR (CONE ESTATE MANSION HOUSE)
An imposing sight nestled into the mountainside, Flat Top Manor is a fine example of what Southern money was all about. A gleaming white staircase leads to a circular porch, which extends along the right side of the mansion. From the porch, a series of striking white columns support the second-story verandah, while a knee-height white railing prefaces the beautiful view of the old carriage route and town of Blowing Rock below. The house is a hive of activity in summer, when hot hikers and equestrians come in off the nearby trails to sit on the porch and admire the panorama.

Call or sign up for the free 30-minute **tour** (☎ 828-295-3782; ☺ 10am, 11am, 2pm, 3pm & 4pm weekends only Jun-Oct) at the visitor center, and admire the unusual dormers, leaded-glass windows and stark white columns up close.

PARKWAY CRAFT CENTER
☎ 828-295-7938; www.southernhighlandguild.org; ☺ 9am-5pm Mar 15-Nov 30
The center is one of five shops of the Southern Highlands Craft Guild, which showcases regional artists' work for the benefit of educating

the public about the area and its resources. You'll find unique pottery designs, intricate woodwork, hand-detailed jewelry and quilts among the treasures here. The goods might be a little pricey, but you're paying for the quality; check out the stained-glass suncatchers for an inexpensive souvenir. The shop is inside Flat Top Manor, across from the visitor center.

JULIAN PRICE MEMORIAL PARK

Map 5; MP 295.1

Perched at the base of Grandfather Mountain, this area sports an exciting assortment of wildlife species, plant life and water activities, as well as three trails covering all difficulty levels. That also means it's a prime destination for families and college students (due to its proximity to Appalachian State University), especially in summer. Amid thickets of vivid wildflowers and rhododendrons, see if you can spot the kooky jack o' lantern mushrooms that supposedly glow in the dark. The park is named for Julian Price, president of the Jefferson Pilot Standard Life Insurance company, which donated this land to the NPS upon Price's death.

The moderate, 4.9-mile **Boone Fork Trail Loop** begins here, among a spacious picnic area that sits by a meandering stream. Beginners enjoy a slight challenge with the 2.7-mile **Price Lake Loop Trail**, which circles the trout-stocked lake – it's best to bring a change of socks for this one, as the trail gets quite wet from close proximity to the lake. The moderate **Green Knob Trail** (aka Lost Cove Ridge Trail) weaves through meadow, arriving at a rickety lookout tower. Bathrooms are available, and leashed pets are allowed.

Price Lake is ahead, on the left-hand side of the Parkway, and a small wooden platform juts into the water for a cool view. Boats without motors and/or sails are permitted; there's a ramp behind the parking area. Visitors can rent boats here.

The largest campground on the Parkway, Price Park (p38), is farther south, on the right-hand side of the road, and there's a small registration center as well as a trash depot, clean water fill-up and public telephones. Backcountry hikers and campers can also pick up permits at the registration center.

On the left-hand side of the road, the **Boone Fork Overlook** offers canoe rentals ($4-6 per hr; ☺ 8:30am-6pm), a small snack shop and a public boat ramp.

At the Boone Fork parking area (MP 300), you can access the Tanawha Trail, as well as the nine trails for Grandfather Mountain (permits are required – purchase them at Grandfather Mountain).

SIGHTS & ACTIVITIES

LINN COVE VIADUCT (MP 304.6)

This manmade wonder provides spectacular views of Grandfather Mountain; it's considered the 'missing link' that finally made the Blue Ridge Parkway complete.

Because of the mountain's rugged nature, heavy equipment and crews would have irreversibly damaged the fragile ecosystem. Hugh Morton, a spunky conservationist, fought for years against the construction of the final segment of the Blue Ridge Parkway around Grandfather Mountain. It was eventually decided that the viaduct would utilize a 'progressive placement' of sections, essentially building each of the seven vertical piers on top of each other. Construction began in 1979 and lasted until 1983; the dedication and opening occurred in 1987. Today visitors don't have to get off at Holloway Rd (US 221) to complete their journey, because the Parkway is one complete 469-mile road.

TANAWHA TRAIL (MP 303)

The newest and most expensive trail along the Parkway does lay claim to unbeatable views. Because the trail lies along the southeastern edge of Grandfather Mountain, the terrain contains a delicate ecosystem of rare plants – which explains the arched bridges and walkways (many flown in via helicopter) that allow hikers to enjoy the natural beauty without disturbing future growth.

Access the 13.5-mile trail from the Beacon Heights parking area, just before the Linn Cove Viaduct. You'll hike a steep set of stone steps underneath the viaduct and past a giant boulder wall while cars whoosh over the bridge. Nearby Wilson Creek gurgles as the path moves through a clearing sprinkled with more boulders until the trail climbs sharply to the best section of the hike, Rough Ridge. Here a 200ft wooden boardwalk leads not over dunes but over the rare sand myrtle plant and wild mountain heather. The 360° view from the 6000ft elevation is breathtaking, especially the sight of the Linn Cove Viaduct.

From the boardwalk you'll move through a forest of dense trees, which opens up to a rock garden of boulders that jut from the earth. Continue through rhododendron patches to the junction of the Daniel Boone Scout Trail (one of the Grandfather Mountain trails – hiking it requires a permit and fee since it's on private land). As you head toward Boone Fork Creek, the terrain can be a bit soggy, so step lightly. The trail crosses more thick walls of rhododendron and trickling cascades until it meets up with a logging road, moves through another hardwood forest and ends up in a field leading to Boone Fork Rd, where it ends at the campground.

SLEEPING

PRICE PARK CAMPGROUND
☎ 828-295-7591; MP 296.9; campsite $14; ☯ May-Oct

The Parkway's largest campground is also one of the prettiest, in close proximity to the Moses H Cone Estate and horse trails. It's also one of two campgrounds where reservations are accepted for one of the 129 **campsites** (☎ 877-444-6777; www.reserveusa.com). Facilities include a pay phone, restrooms with flush toilets, and water but no showers. There's also fishing, hiking trails and a sky-high amphitheater perched precariously at the end of the clouds for entertainment.

GRANDFATHER MOUNTAIN AREA

Map 5; MP 305

Scared of heights? Don't even attempt to enter this **privately run park** (☎ 800-468-7325; www.grandfather.com; adult/child 4-12/senior $12/6/11; ⊗ 8am-6pm spring & fall, to 7pm summer, to 5pm winter) a mile off the Parkway, because the steep, twisty climb is 1 mile of hairpin turns with absolutely no guardrails. However, visitors are well rewarded with camera-ready panoramic shots of Linville Gorge and the mountain itself, especially from the famous Mile-High Swinging Bridge. A scene from the movie *Forrest Gump* was filmed here.

SIGHTS & ACTIVITIES

MILE-HIGH SWINGING BRIDGE

After driving straight up and climbing 50 steps, you've finally arrived at the highest point in North Carolina. The crossing of the precarious bridge may be a bit nerve-wracking, what with children running willy nilly between your legs as you take deep mountain gulps of air – but it's worth it, worth it, worth it! Just don't think about the infamous scene in *Indiana Jones and the Temple of Doom* – thankfully, this bridge is metal, not wood and string, so the only thing falling would be a camera lens or perhaps someone's lunch.

If you can't face the walk, get a great view of the bridge and gorge below from the parking lot.

WILDLIFE HABITATS

In a reverse take on a 'zoo,' visitors are the ones caged here. That's not such a bad idea when viewing bears, cougars and bald eagles in their natural habitats. The viewing platforms are separated by moats and you're more likely to see white-tailed deer than the elusive cougar. Check out the slippery river otters from behind a giant aquarium glass window.

NATURE MUSEUM

A stuffed bear towers over the entrance to this museum, with an

---

Celestial Tunnel Vision

Of the Parkway's 26 stone tunnels, only one can declare its druid-like connection with a famous stone garden in England: In 2003 former computer engineer Bill Carson discovered that the sun rose in perfect alignment with the Little Switzerland Tunnel at MP 333.4. The rest of the tunnels are amazing themselves, considering the amount of work needed to blast through the mountains with limited equipment. Rough Ridge is the shortest, at 150ft, and Pine Mountain is the longest, and spookiest, at 1434ft. Keep those headlights on – it's the law.

assortment of fun and unusual exhibits reminiscent of a North Carolina Ripley's Believe It or Not! Touch a billion-year-old rock, see the finest example of an amethyst discovered in North America and enjoy a selection of cougar and black-bear photos behind glass. It's good for adults and children.

HIKING

Give those calf muscles a workout on one of the four trails. Beginners should stick to the relatively easy 0.4-mile **Woods Walk** or push themselves a little on the **Bridge Trail**, which skirts underneath the bridge and ventures toward stunning rock outcroppings. The **Crest Trails** are the black diamonds of trails here and require strenuous exertion.

SLEEPING & EATING

GRANDFATHER MOUNTAIN CAMPGROUND
☎ 800-788-CLUB; MP 305.1; campsite/cabin $18/109
This makes a good base for exploring Blowing Rock and Boone. To get there, turn onto NC 105 north at MP 305.1.

GRANDFATHER MOUNTAIN SNACK BAR (MP 305)
This'll take you back to your school cafeteria. There's a rather unremarkable snack counter here for a quick bite after exploration (skip the pizza). Shaded picnic areas are scattered throughout.

LINVILLE FALLS

Map 5; MP 316.4
The largest-volume waterfall east of the Mississippi, Linville Falls is probably the most famous waterfall along the entire Parkway – and the crowds prove it. Go on a weekday if possible.

The Linville River begins at Grandfather Mountain, descending 2000ft through the Catawba Valley and a rugged gorge etched over many years. The falls are divided by two sections that used to be the same length, before a portion of the upper falls collapsed onto the lower one in 1900. It's now known as a 'double cascade' and features an unusual effect: Water appears to disappear between the two sections. The lower section is now longer and releases a tremendous misty spray down the gorge.

An access road leads about a mile and a half from the Parkway to Linville Falls and dead-ends at the visitor center.

SIGHTS & ACTIVITIES

VISITOR CENTER
This center may house the worst bathroom on the Parkway, but the staff couldn't be friendlier. A stream parallels the parking area, and shaded picnic tables dot the grass. The best waterfall hike is the 1.6-mile **Falls Trail**, which starts just beyond the visitor center across the

bridge – and judging from the throngs of schoolchildren on the path, it's not a tough-guy trail.

LINVILLE CAVERNS
☎ 800-419-0540; www.linvillecaverns.com; US 221S; adult/child 5-12/senior $5/3/4

North Carolina's only caverns, an underground labyrinth of odd-shaped rock formations, make a great destination for kids. Let them explore the 'bat' cave while you learn the difference between a stalactite and stalagmite. Bring a warm, waterproof jacket, since the cave hovers around a chilly 52°F, with cold drips around every nook. Sure, it's a little hokey, but it's a lot of fun and one of the cheaper attractions around. It's also wheelchair accessible. Be forewarned that the hours vary widely, and heavy rain can close the caverns. Take the Linville Falls exit off the Parkway and follow US 221 south for about 5 miles (entrance is on the right).

LINVILLE GORGE TRAIL (MP 316.4)
For a strenuous 1.4-mile hike to the falls, start at the visitor center

---

DETOUR: PENLAND SCHOOL OF CRAFTS

Like a Salvador Dali painting come to life, this artists' educational retreat abounds with strange and beautiful works of art. Pupils study unique art forms like glassblowing, forged ironworks, bookmaking, and even concrete jewelry and guitar making.

As the Industrial Revolution threatened to wipe out the process of hand weaving on giant wooden looms, one woman (Miss Lucy, as she was known) focused on preserving traditional methods and established the Penland Weavers in this area in 1923. By 1929 word got out about this unique organization, and an official 'school' was established for regional weavers. The artists' mediums grew broader over the years to include metals, glass and elements of the environment, and today the school enjoys an international reputation.

If you're serious about craftsmanship or curious about how to create your own paper (for example), consider taking a class. Programs usually last a week to 2½ weeks, and tuition starts at $2936; scholarships are available.

If you don't have that much time, browse the masterpieces in the eclectic **crafts shop** (☎ 828-765-2359; www.penland.org; ☺ 10am-5pm Tue-Sat, from noon Sun), where prices range from a couple hundred dollars for a mouth-blown glass bowl to a buck for a handmade button.

Penland is a long, twisty drive from the Parkway, but it's worth it. From the Parkway, take NC 226 west toward Spruce Pine. Then take NC 19 south and look for a Texaco station on the left. Directly across from the station, make a right onto Penland Rd and follow for 3 (long) miles. Cross the bridge and railroad tracks, and about 1 mile up, bear left at the big curve and head all the way up the hill.

and go through to the back, where you'll come to a bridge. The **Duggers Creek Trail** goes left, and you can take this for a pretty loop around the creek and see some inspirational sayings nailed to trees throughout. The trail returns to the junction with the Gorge Trail, which then moves right.

It's a gradual ascent for about 0.3 miles to the Plunge Basin Overlook. The overlook path veers to the right; follow it down steep stone steps to a small rocky alcove above the falls. Climb back out and rejoin the Gorge Trail at the top. Turn right and be careful of the slippery rocks on the steep descent. At the bottom, stay to the right and continue descending past a craggy overhang (which makes a good shelter, by the way) to a wet cliff. Keep descending (!), staying to the right until you reach the base. You're finally there when you can see thin rays of sunshine streaming through the canopy and piercing the blue water of the plunge pool – it's a true wilderness feeling. As tempting as the pool is, swimming is not allowed. On the way back, watch your footing here as you'll have to step over slippery rocks to negotiate the trail.

WISEMAN'S VIEW

An amazing detour, Wiseman's View overlooks Hawksbill and Table Rock, as well as one of the wildest gorges in North America. Peregrine falcons and golden eagles can often be seen soaring above the jagged, rocky cliffs.

Go at sunset if you want to catch a glimpse of the mysterious Brown Mountain Lights, which flicker red and blue over Brown Mountain. Cherokee legends mention this phenomenon, but modern-day scientists have no explanation for it.

To get to Wiseman's View, exit the Parkway around Linville Falls (MP 317) and take the misleadingly named Kistler Memorial Hwy (which is actually a rough dirt road) until it turns into a gravel road, and proceed to the end.

SLEEPING

LINVILLE FALLS CAMPGROUND

☎ 828-295-7591; MP 316; campsite $14, ☼ May-Oct

It's the most popular Parkway campground, mainly due to the numerous waterfront campsites. It's also one of two campgrounds where **reservations** (☎ 877-444-6777; www.reserveusa.com) are accepted for one of the 50 sites. Amenities include a visitor center, fishing, flush toilets and water, an amphitheater, access to trails into Linville Gorge and an enormous fireplace with evening campfire programs.

BEAR DEN CAMPGROUND

☎ 828-765-2888; 600 Bear Den Mountain Rd, Spruce Pine; campsite/cabin $28-30/55-210; ☼ camping Mar 1-Nov 30, cabins year-round

One of the best campgrounds around for sheer fun, Bear Den boasts a sandy beach with lake swimming and paddleboat and canoe rentals, a playground, a super-clean bathhouse with hot showers and

How the British Lost America

Don't be surprised to see men in uniform around here...Revolutionary War uniforms, that is. Located in Gillespie Gap, the Museum of North Carolina Minerals marks an important battle that changed the way Yanks would speak forever.

On September 29, 1780, hundreds of Patriot militiamen streamed through the pass on their way to a battle that Thomas Jefferson declared would 'turn the tide of the Revolutionary War.' The Overmountain Men, as they were known, crossed the gap, splitting their numbers and safely making it across. At the same time, British major Patrick Ferguson (under Lord Cornwallis) had orders to head for the Blue Ridge to suppress possible resistance from western militia. On October 7, the Patriots killed Ferguson at the Battle of Kings Mountain and captured and killed his entire force of 1000 men. This devastating defeat ultimately destroyed Britain's hopes for ending the war quickly, and the battle would later be referred to as the 'first link in a chain of evils that led to the loss of America.'

miles of trails. Hit the ATM in the trading post for camp supplies and groceries. To get there, at MP 324.8, turn left onto Bear Den Mountain Rd.

ALTAPASS ORCHARD

Map 5; MP 328.3

So much more than your ordinary apple farm, the **orchard** (☎ 888-765-9531; www.altapassorchard.com; ☯ 10am-6pm late May-late Oct) thrives today despite the area's many near-death experiences.

The Clinchfield Railroad – an engineering marvel of its time, boasting 18 tunnels in a 13-mile stretch – developed this land in the late 1800s as a resort area for rail travelers until a new highway bypassed the gap and turned the place into a ghost town. The railroad sold the land above its tracks to a former employee who planted fruit trees and hired many out-of-work locals to tend to them. But the vibrant orchard began to fade when the construction of the Blue Ridge Parkway divided the property in half after protracted court battles.

Long dormant, this lush treasure turned overgrown mess found a savior in 1995, when Kit Trubey essentially prevented future development by purchasing more than 280 acres. Today Kit's brother and his wife own the orchard and have spearheaded a foundation based on preserving mountain heritage.

An old-timey general store and the occasional live bluegrass jams add to the orchard's atmosphere, and there are also hayrides, storytelling and butterfly tagging for the wee ones. How 'bout them apples?

MUSEUM OF NORTH CAROLINA MINERALS

Map 5; MP 330.9

Four hundred million years ago, after a continental collision forced molten material into the cracks of a dark rock known as gneiss, huge deposits of minerals formed. Today quartz, feldspar, mica and gemstones abound in the southern Appalachians.

Unless you're a miner or geologist, though, this quirky **museum** (☎ 828-765-2761; ✆ 9am-5pm) may be your only opportunity to see the area's rich mineral resources in their pure forms, including copper, iron, quartz and mica. Ever wonder what a silica tetrahedron looks like? Here's your chance. Kids can poke around the hands-on exhibits, learning which minerals glow in the dark, working a morphing rock machine and seeing petrified wood up close.

The **Mitchell County Chamber of Commerce** (☎ 800-227-3912) operates a small information counter inside the museum.

CRABTREE MEADOWS

Map 5; MP 339

It's speculated that the open meadows here may have been created by Native Americans, who burned the vegetation to make their hunting easier. Today, the area crawls more with visitors than wildlife, but it's a great base to explore the southern end of the Blue Ridge Mountains – don't miss it in spring, when it explodes with blankets of wildflowers.

SIGHTS & ACTIVITIES

CRABTREE FALLS LOOP TRAIL (MP 339.5)

The length of this journey to see one of the prettiest waterfalls along the Parkway will depend on whether you hike back after viewing the falls or continue on the loop. Start out in the campground area of the Crabtree Falls Visitor Center and walk down the wide path of primitive steps. At the bottom is a fork – go right.

On your steep descent, you're likely to see colorful salamanders enjoying the many wet-weather springs. The trail is slippery in places, with standing water hiding sharp rocks, and it is cut around extremely rocky ground. There are three steep and narrow stone staircases; the first one takes an angled curve to the bottom, and the next two are slippery and steeper. Fortunately, a few benches help ease the pain.

The loud rush of the falls signals your approach, and once you navigate a treacherous, narrow section, cascading water roars off the 60ft rock cliff en route to the rocks below. A small wooden bridge provides the best picture-taking opportunities, with a built-in bench where you can rest and admire. Continue across the bridge for the rest of the 1.6-mile loop that levels out after a short, strenuous hike upward, meandering across Crabtree Creek and into the parking area.

SLEEPING & EATING

CRABTREE MEADOWS CAMPGROUND
☎ 828-765-6082; MP 339.5; campsite $14; ✷ May-Oct

Crabtree Meadows is an underused campground on the Parkway (which is almost unheard of), so take advantage of the solitude – on some evenings, you can even hear the faint roar of Crabtree Falls. Facilities include a snack and gift shop, restrooms, flush toilets and water, trails and an amphitheater for campfire programs.

CRABTREE MEADOWS SNACK BAR

What used to be a small, full-service restaurant is now a quick snack shop inside the gift shop. Boxed lunches (sandwiches are made fresh daily), fruit, energy bars, drinks and even ice cream are available to help you fuel up before – or quench your thirst after – the big falls hike. The couple who run the snack-gift shop are probably the nicest concessionaires along the Parkway.

MT MITCHELL STATE PARK

Map 5; MP 355

The highest peak in the Black Mountains (6684ft) and east of the Mississippi River, Mt Mitchell boasts an intriguing history involving a mathematical controversy and an accidental death.

In the mid-1800s Grandfather Mountain was believed to be the highest peak in the southeastern US. But a science professor at the University of North Carolina, Elisha Mitchell, believed the Black Mountains were higher. He started measuring the peaks in the Carolina and Black Mountains and declared a peak with an elevation of 6672ft – 708ft higher than Grandfather.

A dispute arose in 1855 when Mitchell butted measuring sticks with US senator Thomas Lanier Clingman, who claimed to have been the first one to measure the highest peak in the Black Mountains. Mitchell, determined to verify his own measurements, embarked on a return trip to the Black Mountains in 1857, with his son, daughter and a servant. On the afternoon of June 27, a Saturday, Mitchell said he was going to check on the Caney River settlement and would return on Monday. This was the last time his son saw him alive. It wasn't until Thursday that Mitchell was deemed missing, and upon retracing his steps, the search team encountered a 40ft waterfall. It looked as if a piece of its dangerous precipice had been ripped away, and when the team peered over the waterfall into its deep pool, they saw Mitchell's body. Originally buried in Asheville, his remains now lie atop the mountain on which he lost his life, and which is now named in his honor (his grave is near the foot of the observation tower). In 1915 Mt Mitchell became North Carolina's first state park.

As for Thomas Clingman, he settled for second place, with Clingmans Dome in the Great Smokies.

Today the **park** (☎ 828-675-4611; www.ils.unc.edu/parkproject/

visit/momi/info.html; ☯ 8am-6pm Nov-Feb, to 7pm Mar & Oct, to 8pm April & Sept, to 9pm May-Aug), on NC 128 off the Parkway, is a perpetually misty overlook with chilly temperatures, though the rangers say it's the best place to watch a sunrise or sunset – that is, when you can actually see the sun. In September 2004, landslides caused by storms restricted access to the park; the roads were to be reopened within the year, but check the website to be sure.

SIGHTS & ACTIVITIES

OBSERVATION TOWER
Feeling lightheaded? It's no wonder – you're 1¼ miles above sea level here. Despite the lofty perch, though, you'll be hard pressed to see much; mist obscures the view 90% of the time. However, at the first signs of the sun peeking through, make a run for the space-agey tower to take in a spectacular, 85-miles-in-any-direction vista, and linger for the legendary sunsets.

EXHIBIT HALL
☯ 10am-6pm May-Oct, weather permitting
Near the mountain's summit, the hall contains dioramas and topographic maps, a reproduction of Elisha Mitchell's cabin and a lifesize model of 'Big Tom,' a legendary bear hunter in these parts who led the search for Mitchell upon his disappearance. There's also an interactive weather station where you can plug in your vitals and read about the weather conditions on your birthdate.

SLEEPING & EATING

Hardy types can camp and eat at Mt Mitchell State Park itself, while the nearby town of Burnsville makes a good base with more comfortable accommodations. In the evening, watch a flick in retro seating at the historic **Yancey Theatre** (☎ 877-678-3322; 119 W Main St, Burnsville; $5).

MT MITCHELL STATE PARK CAMPGROUND
☎ 828-675-4611; campsite $9/15 Nov 1-Apr 30/May 1-Oct 31
The nine tent sites should suffice for brave, thick-skinned campers (no hot water or showers provided). Otherwise, make it a day trip and enjoy a mile-high picnic nestled up to the fireplaces in the two shelters. Don't forget to grab a sweater or windproof jacket if you're jaunting up to the tower – temperatures can be 10 to 15 degrees cooler than on the Parkway, and winds have been clocked at 100mph. Restrooms are available.

MT MITCHELL STATE PARK RESTAURANT
☎ 828-675-9545; meals $3-15; ☯ May-Oct
The food isn't much to write home about, but the prices are cheap and we're surprised they don't tack on a surcharge for the incredible view. Warm up in front of the wood-burning fireplace.

NU-WRAY INN

☎ 828-628-2329; www.nuwrayinn.com; Town Square, Burnsville; d $65-85

Located off the Parkway in tiny Burnsville, the inn is a multilevel Victorian mishmash, reminiscent of a traditional boardinghouse along a well-traveled route. Its seasoned past has fueled the stories about guests' so-called 'sightings' of previous residents. The creaky front porch and 2nd-floor verandah boast cozy rocking chairs and a perfect view of Burnsville's historic town square. Rates include breakfast. Take NC 80 west to US 19E south.

CLEAR CREEK RANCH

☎ 800-651-4510; 100 Clear Creek Dr, Burnsville; adult/child 5-12/child 2-5 $205/135/40 daily, $1350/850/250 weekly; ☾ Apr 1-Dec 1

Give in to your *City Slickers* desires at Clear Creek Ranch, where you can wrangle a weekly stay for family-style eats, marshmallow roasts and nightly hootenannies by the river.

Around MP 343 on the Parkway, take NC 80 west about 3 miles and turn right on Clear Creek Rd.

CRAGGY GARDENS

Map 6; MP 364.6

A great place to marvel at the wildflowers is the **Craggy Gardens Trail** (MP 364.5). Look out for Indian pipe, bee balm, spiderwort, Turk's cap lily, jewel weed, fire pink, dodder and dozens of other varieties in a hundred different colors. Other good hikes range from 0.5-mile strolls to 4-mile adventures. Breathtaking vistas await.

The **visitor center** here is arguably the Parkway's best, thanks to its sprawling view of the mountains, valley, wildflowers and tunnels. There's always a crowd on both sides of the parking lot snapping photos of the incredible panoramic vistas, so be careful when passing through. Restrooms are available.

FOLK ART CENTER

Map 6; MP 382

Part of the Southern Highlands Craft Guild, the **center** (☎ 828-298-7928; ☾ 9am-6pm Apr-Dec, to 5pm Jan-Mar) showcases unique local craftsmanship in its gallery of permanent and rotating exhibits. An adjacent building, which will house more interpretive exhibits, is under construction and scheduled to open by 2007.

The term 'gift shop' seems inadequate to describe the long gallery of beautiful crafts for sale. Intricate jewelry using gems mined from local quarries, complex basket weaves, detailed patchwork quilts, silky scarves and smooth wooden carvings merely scratch the surface of what's available here. If you're interested in seeing how these unique gifts take shape, ask about the live demonstrations (such as broom-making) in the lobby.

There's also a small, NPS-staffed information center here. Consider buying a bluegrass CD to keep you in the mood as you travel down the Parkway.

ON THE ROAD

Tucked off a side road from the Parkway, the **Blue Ridge Parkway Headquarters** (☎ 828-298-0398; www.nps.gov/blri; MP 382, mailing address: 199 Hemphill Knob Rd, Asheville, NC 28803; ☻ 8am-4:30pm Mon-Fri) is primarily an administrative office, and the reception desk is unmanned. There are a few maps and brochures if you're in dire need, but you'll be better off browsing the plethora of pamphlets at the Folk Art Center.

The **Mountains-to-Sea Trail (MTS)** is accessible from the parking lot; this proposed grand hiking trail is designed to rival the Appalachian Trail, stretching from the mountains to North Carolina's coast. Still not completed, the trail roughly parallels the Parkway at Doughton Park down to the Oconaluftee Visitor Center (MP 469.1). For more information, including maps of the work-in-progress, visit www.ncmst.org.

LAKE POWHATAN

Map 6; MP 393.7

Feeling hot? Go jump in a lake – you can take your pick from thirteen of 'em at the **Lake Powhatan Recreation Area** (☎ 828-670-5627; 375 Wesley Branch Rd; ☻ mid-Mar–late Oct). At MP 393.7, take NC 191 west to Bent Creek Branch Rd (NC 3480) and follow signs to the recreation area.

Families and single travelers will love this bustling outdoor playground with ample fishing, mountain biking, swimming and hiking activities. Non-motorized boating is allowed. It's a favorite with mountain bikers for its exciting network of single-track and forest-road trails, as well as with anglers for the abundant rainbow and brown trout. Varied hiking trails, ranging from the Mountains-to-Sea Trail to an old route toward the Biltmore Estate, challenge and entertain hikers along the border of Pisgah National Forest. You will see bears here – some trails pass through a bear sanctuary, and researchers like to collect data in the area.

Pretty **Lake Powhatan Campground** (☎ 877-444-6777; campsite $15; ☻ 7am-10pm mid-May–late Oct) puts you in proximity to mountain biking, hiking and lake swimming. Weekends require a two-night minimum, and showers are available.

ASHEVILLE

Population 69,000; Map 9

Asheville's boosters exhort you to refer to their exceedingly pleasant western North Carolina city as the 'Paris of the South.' Perhaps they've never seen the bright lights of Paris. Notwithstanding, their enthusiasm for Asheville's bohemian pleasures is not misplaced. By day the streets are filled with hipsters perusing the used clothing shops or comparing tattoos; at night the sweet-smelling mountain air is graced with the sounds of musicians tuning their

DETOUR: BLACK MOUNTAIN

Quintessential 'small-town America' at its most eclectic is the best way to describe this bohemian town. If you have an extra day, spend it here, especially at the Inn on Mill Creek, where the twisty drive off the Parkway is an adventure in itself. To get to Black Mountain from the Parkway, take NC 80 east and prepare for at least a half-hour, hairpin-turn drive down from the mountains until you hit US 70. Take that south into Old Fort and follow the signs for I-40 to Black Mountain.

The Inn on Mill Creek (☎ 877-735-2964, 828-668-1115; www.inn-on-mill-creek.com; d $110-175) is a favorite retreat of ours. It's a beautiful lakefront home with enormous yet cozy Jacuzzi suites, an onsite apple-apricot-peach orchard with blackberry and raspberry thickets, and gourmet breakfasts that put Martha Stewart to shame. There are even hiking and biking trails and in-room massages for those achy muscles afterward. Innkeepers Jim and Aline really go out of their way to take care of guests – they have to. There's no one around for miles, and that's the best part: It's a true mountain getaway. Don't forget to ask about the mysterious 'Geyser Geezer' before you leave.

What do you get when you throw together New Orleans, Victorian England and Grandma's attic? The decor for **Madisons** (☎ 828-669-4785; 10 Florida Ave; meals $10-24), a wild restaurant tucked inside a residential area that you might otherwise have just passed by. The chicken marsala is heavenly. Ask to sit in the library alcove.

instruments as the many clubs and cafes open their doors to showcase the local music scene.

More than a century ago, millionaire George Vanderbilt raved that Asheville was the 'most beautiful land in the world.' Whatever your means, it's hard not to be impressed with this surprisingly liberal town, which retains a certain 1920s charm in a fabulous setting. Don't be surprised if you extend your stay, just as Vanderbilt did.

To get to Asheville, you can either take US 70 (just south of the Folk Art Center) to I-240 or wait until you pass the Park Headquarters, and take I-40 to I-240. This Southern belle of a city makes a great base for exploring the southern portion of the Parkway and the Great Smoky Mountains.

HISTORY

In the late 1700s Asheville was but a crossing of two Indian trails when homesteaders from Northern Ireland dubbed the valley 'Eden land.' A real-estate broker developed the area, and tiny Asheville was founded in 1797 and named after North Carolina governor Samuel Ashe. At first the town became not a resort but a stopover for cattle farmers driving their herds to market. Growth was slow in those early, mud-caked years.

↓ NORTH CAROLINA ASHEVILLE

Asheville remained a backwater until the railroad came to town in 1880. Virtually overnight, the place was transformed, as trains chugged in thousands of tourists from the East Coast and beyond. One carriage carried 26-year-old George Vanderbilt, heir to a vast railway fortune, and the rugged beauty of the region opened both his heart and wallet. Vanderbilt purchased 125,000 acres of land, stretching from Asheville to the present-day Pisgah National Forest, and in 1890 he asked Richard Morris Hunt to draw up plans for the Biltmore House. Hundreds of artisans and builders from Europe would spend six years fashioning the interior and exterior of this grand chateau, now the largest private residence in the world.

In recent years Asheville has regained much of its Jazz Age allure. Dozens of architectural gems have been restored, and the crisp mountain air now draws a varied crowd of bohemians, outdoors enthusiasts and retirees. Fortunately, mutual tolerance is in ample supply, and a good time is had by all.

ORIENTATION & INFORMATION

At the confluence of the Swannanoa and French Broad Rivers, Asheville sits in the middle of a loop formed by I-40 and I-240. The town is relatively compact and easy to negotiate on foot. The sprawling Biltmore Estate lies on its southern boundary.

The **visitor center** (☎ 828-258-6101, 800-257-1300; www.explore asheville.com; 151 Haywood St; ☯ 8:30am-5:30pm Mon-Fri, 9am-5pm Sat & Sun) run by the Chamber of Commerce, is at exit 4C off I-240. Its excellent website is chock-full of information on sights, activities and lodging and dining options, plus an events calendar and a helpful itinerary planner.

Malaprop's Bookstore & Café (☎ 828-254-6734; 55 Haywood St; ☯ 9am-9pm Mon-Thu, until 10pm Fri & Sat, until 6pm Sun) is an excellent place to pick up regional maps and travel books; join the cappuccino-sipping bohemians. Bring your laptop for free wireless access.

The main **post office** is at 33 Coxe Ave. The **public library** (☎ 828-251-4991; 67 Haywood Ave; ☯ 10am-8pm Mon-Thu, until 6pm Fri, until 5pm Sat) offers free Internet access.

The **Mission St Joseph's Hospital** (☎ 828-213-1111; 509 Biltmore Ave) has a 24-hour emergency ward, plus walk-in care services from noon to 10pm. **Midtown Family Medicine and Urgent Care** (☎ 828-232-1555; 120B Patton Ave; ☯ 11am-5pm Mon-Fri, 10am-2pm Sun) is adjacent to Days Inn. It's a drop-in clinic for non-life-threatening emergencies.

The *Asheville Citizen-Times* (www.citizen-times.com) is the biggest daily newspaper in western North Carolina. The *Mountain Xpress* (www.mountainxpress.com), a free independent weekly paper available in local bars and restaurants, is the place to look for nightlife and entertainment listings.

Three public **parking garages** serve downtown; parking is free for the first hour and $0.50 per hour thereafter.

SIGHTS & ACTIVITIES

BILTMORE ESTATE

☎ 828-255-1333, 800-624-1575; www.biltmore.com; 1 Approach Rd; adult/child 6-16 $39/19.50; ⏱ 9am-4pm Jan-Mar 14, 8:30am-5pm Mar 15-Dec 31

With 250 rooms, the gorgeous, sprawling Biltmore Estate is overwhelmingly sumptuous in scale and decoration. Built for the filthy-rich Vanderbilt family as a holiday home, the 1895 mansion is styled after a French chateau. George Vanderbilt quaintly referred to the charming behemoth as his 'cottage.' Many visitors recognize the grounds from the film *Being There*, starring the late great Peter Sellers. The author Henry James complained during a 1905 visit that his bedroom was at least a half-mile from the library. Be sure to save time for the cavernous basement, which housed the bowling alley, swimming pool, kitchen and servants' quarters.

Plan to spend quite a few hours viewing the estate to justify the hefty admission charges. The Biltmore's winery offers tastings and sales. Mid-price meals are available at several venues, and the gift shop is the size of a small supermarket.

THOMAS WOLFE MEMORIAL

☎ 828-253-8304; 52 N Market St; adult/student $1/0.50; ⏱ 9am-5pm Tue-Sat, 1-5pm Sun

The local literary landmark, the Thomas Wolfe Memorial is an early-1900s boardinghouse that provided the setting for Wolfe's epic autobiographical novel, *Look Homeward, Angel*. The author described the rambling clapboard structure as an 'old dilapidated house with 18 or 20 drafty, high-ceilinged rooms.' (The 1929 novel was peppered with sometimes unflattering local color, and its references incensed so many locals that the public library banned it for seven years.) In 1998 an arson attack on the old house unleashed an enormously destructive blaze that devoured many original artifacts and caused widespread devastation. Following a costly renovation effort, 2004 marked the grand reopening of the house as a museum and visitor center.

BOTANICAL GARDENS

☎ 828-252-5190; 151 Weaver Blvd; admission free; ⏱ dawn-dusk

On a 10-acre site north of downtown, the Botanical Gardens offer a year-round show of blossoms, buds, fruits or leaves, depending on the season. The displays of Appalachian plants and flowers are a botanist's dream, but anyone will enjoy a stroll on shady, leaf-covered paths beneath giant sycamores and along babbling brooks. There's a Garden for the Blind with labels in Braille. The gardens are off Broadway next to the UNC-Asheville campus.

CLIMBMAX INDOOR CLIMBING CENTER

☎ 828-252-9996; 43 Wall St; indoor bouldering/rope climbing $8.50/12.50; ⏱ 3:30-10pm Tue & Thu, noon-10pm Wed & Fri, 10am-10pm Sat, 1-6pm Sun

Scale the heights at the full-service climbing center, or head to the hills on a rock-climbing excursion with an expert guide (from $165).

BIO-WHEELS

☎ 888-881-2453, 828-232-0300; www.biowheels.com; 76 Biltmore Ave; tours half day/full day $85-150/140-250; ☺ 10am-6:30pm Mon-Sat, 1-5pm Sun

This excellent operation is the best regional provider for outdoor cycling activities. In addition to rentals, sales and service, Bio-Wheels offers guided excursions, including leisurely sunset rides along the Parkway and mountain bike tours, such as the intermediate-level Epic Backwoods Ride. Tours are priced according to group size.

INNER MOUNTAIN CAVING EXPLORATIONS

☎ 866-444-7935; www.innermtnexplorer.com; 85 Ed DeBruhl Hill Rd, Alexander

Going underground is the only way you're going to see what's underneath that mountain. This unique group leads expeditions to underground lakes, rivers and waterfalls. Each trip is fully outfitted with safety gear, but you must bring good hiking boots and appropriate clothing for cool temperatures. Trips range from a three-hour subterranean stroll tailored for beginners ($58) to the six-hour Adventurer Trip ($95) for folks who live to wallow in the mud; there's even an overnight trip ($190). It's enough to make any neophyte spelunker test the echo with a lusty shout of 'Cowabunga!' Inner Mountain is in Alexander, 12 miles northeast of Asheville off US 77/25.

SLEEPING

Prices listed reflect summer high-season rates; note that prices really jump in October, at the height of the leaf-peeping season. Asheville is justifiably famous for its B&Bs; many of them are housed in impressive Jazz Age houses. **Asheville Bed & Breakfast Association** (☎ 828-252-0200, 877-262-6867; www.ashevillebba.com) handles bookings for 21 B&Bs in the Asheville area, from Victorian mansions to mountain retreats.

Chain motels cluster north of downtown at Merrimon Ave, with rates averaging $50 to $60. East on Tunnel Rd at I-240 exit 6 are some independent places, such as the nondescript **Blue Ridge Motor Lodge** (☎ 828-254-0805; 60 Tunnel Rd; r $40-60; Ⓟ ⊠).

BEAR CREEK CAMPGROUND

☎ 828-253-0798, 81 S Bear Creek Rd; campsite with/without electricity $28/25, RV site $31; ☺ year-round

Right next to the Biltmore Estate, this campground contains full facilities (clubhouse, laundry, pool etc), RV sites with hookups and nice tent sites. If you're going westbound on I-40, take exit 47 and proceed from the signal to the campground; eastbound, take exit 47 and turn right at the signal and left again into S Bear Creek Rd.

ASHEVILLE EAST KOA

☎ 800-562-5907, 828-686-3121; 102 US 70E, Swannanoa; RV site $27-30, suite with kitchen $110, rustic cabin $45-60

Ten miles east of town, this campground offers a range of accommodations, from sites to suites. Take I-40 exit 59, drive north one block to the signal, turn right on US 70 and go 2 miles.

MOUNTAINEER INN
☎ 828-254-5331, 800-255-4080; 155 Tunnel Rd; r from $45

Get a taste of the local color at this spot, which features a towering neon hillbilly sign and cedar-walled rooms.

FOREST MANOR INN
☎ 828-274-3531; www.forestmanorinn.com; 866 Hendersonville Rd; r $89-169

Located near the Biltmore Estate, this charming and immaculate 21-unit motel sits on 4 acres of landscaped, wooded grounds. The good-quality Wildflower Restaurant is adjacent; complimentary continental breakfast is provided.

WRIGHT INN & CARRIAGE HOUSE
☎ 828-251-0789, 800-552-5724; www.wrightinn.com; 235 Pearson Dr; r $99-200, carriage house $200-230

This is how a bed-and-breakfast should be: richly decorated period rooms, wine and cheese afternoons on the wraparound porch and a superb breakfast at a long antique table. A carriage house in the back is available for families or romantics. It's a refreshing walk to downtown Asheville.

From downtown, take Haywood St to Montford Ave and turn right. At Watauga St, turn left and proceed to the end of the street.

RENAISSANCE ASHEVILLE HOTEL
☎ 828-252-8211, fax 828-236-9616; 1 Thomas Wolfe Plaza; high/low season $139/105

Downtown, this 12-story high rise with excellent mountain views offers singles or doubles in Marriott-style luxury. A standard buffet breakfast is included in the price. The hotel houses a large fitness center.

GROVE PARK INN RESORT
☎ 828-252-2711, 800-438-5800; www.groveparkinn.com; 290 Macon Ave; r from $209

As fancy as all get-out, this excellent hotel occupies a classic Arts and Crafts building from 1913. It's famous for its 510 gorgeous rooms and also boasts a fitness center, tennis courts, spa and four restaurants. Prices – always high – fluctuate wildly, depending on the season.

From downtown, take Charlotte St south to Macon Ave, turn left, and go about 2 miles.

INN ON BILTMORE ESTATE
☎ 828-225-1660, 800-922-0084; 1 Antler Hill Rd; r $259-2000

A stunning option on Vanderbilt's property, this world-class resort rests its reputation on a meticulous attention to detail. You can expect to be pampered with fluffy robes and warmed slippers, turn-down service and chocolates left on your pillow (if this is their idea of seduction, it works!). The service and atmosphere are surprisingly down to earth and casual. Many of the rooms boast a gorgeous view of the Great Smokies, marble counters and separate tubs and showers. Don't miss the wonderful breakfast buffet on the terrace overlooking the mountains and the Biltmore house in the distance.

EATING

For a small city, Asheville has an astonishingly good cuisine scene. Loosen your belt and linger over something delicious.

CAFÉ SOLEIL

☎ 828-650-1140; 62 N Lexington Ave; dishes $3-10; ⏲ 11:30am-10pm Tue-Wed, 11:30am-1:30am Thu-Sat, 10am-3pm Sun

This classy and cozy crêperie serves 'em savory and sweet in a pleasant dining room painted in sun-baked hues. Excellent soups and salads and a great wine list make this one of Asheville's most enjoyable restaurants. Friday and Saturday evenings feature live music – klezmer, gypsy and jazz.

BLUE MOON BAKERY

☎ 828-252-6060; 60 Biltmore Ave; lunch $4-7; ⏲ 7:30am-4pm

This cooperatively run bakery serves wholesome, well-conceived sandwiches: Try the Mango Magic with smoked turkey, Swiss cheese and piquant mango chutney. Also tempting are the fresh salads and soups.

MAX & ROSIE'S

☎ 828-254-5352; www.maxandrosies.com; 52 N Lexington Ave; lunch $4-7; ⏲ 11am-5pm Mon-Sat

For your health, this little place serves well-priced veggie burgers, pitas, salads, fresh-squeezed fruit juices and tonics.

RIO BURRITO

☎ 828-253-2422; 11 Broadway; burritos $4.50-6; ⏲ 11:30am-7:30pm Tue-Sat

This nouvelle burrito joint rolls 'em up California-style (that is to say, hot and hefty). If it suits your temperament, try the 'nerve gas' salsa, made from sweet potatoes, peaches and habañero peppers smoked in-house.

TUPELO HONEY CAFÉ

☎ 828-255-4863; 12 College St; breakfast $6-13, dinner $8-12; ⏲ 9am-3pm Tue-Thu, 9am-3pm & 5pm-3am Fri & Sat, 9am-3pm Sun

This pleasant eatery extols the virtues of 'Southern home cooking with an uptown twist.' The amazing breakfasts include a standout called Eggs Crawley: two seared crab cakes topped with poached eggs and hollandaise. It's richer than Vanderbilt.

DOC CHEY'S NOODLE HOUSE

☎ 828-252-8220; 37 Biltmore Ave; noodle bowls & rice plates $6-8; ⏲ 11:30am-10pm Sun-Thu, 11:30am-11pm Fri & Sat

A cheerful interior with bright red walls and vibrant decor is the perfect complement for the steaming bowls of tasty noodles that emerge from the kitchen.

THE MARKET PLACE

☎ 828-252-4162; 20 Wall St; dinner $8-32; ⏲ dinner 5:30-11pm Mon-Sat

Forget the hemp and incense – this earthy venue delivers organic goodness to all with a creative menu that changes seasonally, using local organic ingredients, game and grains straight from the Carolina mountains. Extraordinarily high ceilings and splashy artwork kick it up a notch. Try the $25 prix-fixe Rose Plate Special meal.

THIBODAUX JONES KITCHEN & MEANTIME LOUNGE
☎ 828-225-3065; 48 Biltmore Ave; dishes $8-20; ☽ dinner 5-10pm Tue-Sat, lounge 5pm-close Mon-Sat
The Creole-inspired kitchen of this lively place sends out delicious dishes inspired by the hot jazz music of New Orleans. Don't miss the New Orleans–style barbecue shrimp, sautéed in spicy sherry and garlic herb sauce. There's live music Thursday to Sunday.

BARLEY'S TAPROOM
☎ 828-255-0504; 42 Biltmore Ave; pizzas $12-15; ☽ 11:30am-2am Mon-Sat, noon-midnight Sun
This cavernous place is famous for beer and music, but the tap room also serves uncommonly good bar food, including pizzas, sandwiches and calzones. Come for live music four nights a week.

FRENCH BROAD FOOD CO-OP
☎ 828-255-7650; 90 Biltmore Ave; ☽ 9am-9pm Mon-Sat, noon-8pm Sun
This sweet-smelling grocery store sells organic produce and bulk and natural foods. Vegetarians may want to stock up here before hitting the road again.

ENTERTAINMENT & SHOPPING

Asheville has a rich music scene and plenty of good bars. To find out what's going on, pick up a copy of the free alternative weekly *Mountain Xpress* or the *Smoky Mountain News*.

THE ORANGE PEEL SOCIAL AID & PLEASURE CLUB
☎ 828-225-5851; www.theorangepeel.net; 101 N Biltmore Ave; ☽ vary
Quality funk, punk and alt-country acts do their thing at this most excellent music hall.

SMOKEY AFTER DARK
☎ 828-253-2155; 18 Broadway; ☽ 4pm-2am Sun-Fri, noon-2am Sat
This gay bar still retains the ambience of its roadhouse origins. It's got pool tables and people in-the-know.

FINE ARTS THEATRE
☎ 828-232-1536; 36 Biltmore Ave
The latest art house films are screened here.

BEAN STREETS COFFEE HOUSE
☎ 828-255-8180; 3 Broadway; ☽ 7:30am-6pm Mon-Wed, 7:30am-midnight Thu-Sat, 7:30am-10pm Sun
This well-loved coffeehouse with free wireless Internet access is a

great place to hang out, in spite of the occasional open-mic poetry readings.

MAST GENERAL STORE
☎ 828-232-1883; 15 Biltmore Ave; ☺ 10am-6pm Mon-Thu, 10am-9pm Fri-Sat, noon-5pm Sun

A spinoff from the well-known shop in Boone (p34), this old-fashioned downtown emporium recalls the halcyon early days of the American department store. Downstairs is a complete outfitters department featuring hiking and camping gear, boots and casual footwear.

MT PISGAH

Map 6; MP 407.6

South of Asheville, the Blue Ridge Parkway winds into the **Pisgah National Forest**. Railway magnate George Vanderbilt's purchase of 125,000 acres included **Mt Pisgah** (5749ft), at MP 407.6. A good 1½ mile trail leads up to the peak from the parking lot of the Pisgah Inn. The mountain takes its name from a smaller peak near the Dead Sea in Jordan; the biblical reference tells of a mountain overlooking a 'sprawling land of milk and honey,' which visitors to this area found appropriate. And the view is heavenly, especially from the observation deck of George's old hunting lodge, the modern Pisgah Inn, home to one of the few restaurants where what you see out the window is just as appealing as what you see on your plate.

There's a large campground across from the inn, as well as a camping supply store, bathrooms and, lo and behold, even Internet access ($2 for 20 minutes) in the inn's lobby.

SLEEPING & EATING

MT PISGAH CAMPGROUND
☎ 828-648-2644; MP 408.8; campsite $14; ☺ May-Oct

You're really sleeping in the clouds here at the Parkway's highest campground. The NPS took over operations in 2004 and has upped the number of existing sites to 147. Make sure to bring appropriate clothing for extremely chilly nights. Facilities include food services (at Pisgah Inn), a camp store, flush toilets, water and an amphitheater for campfire programs.

PISGAH INN
☎ 828-235-8228; www.pisgahinn.com; MP 408.6; s/d $80-90, extra person $8, rollaway bed $8; ☺ Mar 29-Nov 1

An extremely popular venue, the inn offers recently renovated rooms with balconies overlooking its famous namesake. And hey, it's one of the few places TV junkies can get their fixes in the mountains. An adjacent restaurant serves three meals a day. Reservations are accepted up to two years in advance for the super-deluxe 'Pisgah Room,' with a fireplace, living room and big-screen TV. ADA Compliant rooms are available upon request

PISGAH INN RESTAURANT

☎ 828-235-8228; ☻ breakfast 7:30-10:30am, lunch 11:30am-4pm, dinner 5-9pm; dishes $2-23

Floor-to-ceiling windows offer extraordinary views of the mountains. The traditional Southern menu features pretty standard choices with a few surprises: black bean hummus, filet mignon and fried green tomatoes.

ON THE ROAD

A favorite kid (or kid-at-heart) activity just off the Parkway, **Sliding Rock** (☎ 828-877-3350; $1) is a must on hot summer days. It's exactly what the name implies – a naturally smooth 'sliding rock' that's been developed into a 60ft waterslide, plunging riders into a chilly 7ft pool. It's hard to resist the refreshment – even Lassie slid down once in her TV series. No tubes are needed here, but do your butt a favor and wear an old pair of jeans, as the surface is tough on swimsuits. Smaller children need to slide with mom or dad. Don't want to get wet? Check out the squeals of laughter from two observation decks. Sliding Rock is open year-round, but the restrooms, changing rooms and lifeguards are available Memorial Day to Labor Day only.

To get there, from the intersection of US 276 and US 64 in Pisgah Forest, go about 8 miles east on US 276. You will pass Looking Glass Falls on the right after 5 miles. Look for signs directing you to the Sliding Rock Recreation Area parking lot on the left.

Several minor sights beckon in the forest to the south of Mt Pisgah. At MP 412, the **Cold Mountain Overlook** affords a view of the 6030ft peak popularized in Charles Frazier's noteworthy novel. The fact that Hollywood did not shoot any scenes for the movie *Cold Mountain* here still rubs locals the wrong way. Near the same spot you'll see a turnoff for US 276 east, which leads to the **Cradle of Forestry in America** (☎ 828-877-3130; adult/child 4-17 $5/2.50; ☻ mid-Apr–early Nov), the country's first forestry school, founded in 1898 by Vanderbilt. It's a good spot to take kids, with live demonstrations of basket-weaving (among other things) and a short film. The guided tours through the surrounding woods are more interesting for grownups. At MP 412, take US 276 toward Brevard about 4 miles and follow signs for the Cradle.

North Carolina contains no fewer than 300 waterfalls, and this region is renowned for them. About a mile southeast of the forestry school on US 276, **Looking Glass Falls** is a 30ft-wide watery curtain that cascades 60ft into a ridiculously clear pool, accessible by a short set of steps.

Southwest of the forest and straddling the South Carolina border, the magnificent cascades of **Whitewater Falls** are definitely worth a detour. The two-tiered falls tumble 411ft down a craggy mass; they're higher than Niagara Falls (but quite a bit narrower). From Brevard, take US 64 southwest for about 23 miles to NC 281 and turn south. Or consider seeing the falls on a three-hour **horse-**

This bucolic little town 40 minutes north of Asheville is a wonderful place to relax and soak up the scenery while also soaking yourself. The hot springs that earned the town its name were discovered by explorers in 1788 (although the Cherokee had been savvy to their existence for centuries).

In 1828 the **Buncombe Turnpike** – the first superhighway of the South – was completed. This road, which connected Tennessee and Kentucky to the East Coast, brought farmers and thousands of horses, cattle and other livestock through town (but only the farmers were allowed to take in the waters). James Patton of Asheville bought the springs in 1831 and by 1837 had built the 350-room Warm Springs Hotel, which featured 13 tall columns commemorating the first colonies. Because of its size and grandeur, it was called Patton's White House. It burned to the ground in 1920.

Today, Hot Springs is a quiet place, save for the contented sighs of pleasure floating on the breeze from the direction of the spa. The town also has several charming B&Bs and a good restaurant or two. Visit Hot Springs' web site (www.hotspringsnc.org) to learn more.

Pamper your weary traveler's bones at the **Hot Springs Spa & Campground** (☎ 828-622-7676; 315 Bridge St; regular/riverside/deluxe campsite $10/20/25, cabin from $40; ☾ 9am-11pm), a backwoods spa 35 miles northwest of Asheville. Curative mineral baths in secluded outdoor settings start at $10 per hour; well-priced massage ($55 per hour) is also available. The campground is a pleasant, sprawling affair on the banks of the French Broad River.

The **Bluff Mountain Festival** (☎ 828-689-5507; www.main.nc.us/bluff; admission free), held in mid-June every year, showcases some of the region's best traditional and bluegrass music. Attendees camp at the Hot Springs Campground and soak at the spa, enjoying great music and a nightly square dance. It's a hoot!

From Asheville, take US 19/23 north from I-240, following signs to Mars Hill and Weaverville. Follow US 25/70 past Marshall and continue on the two-lane road as the highway takes a left turn over Laurel River toward Hot Springs and Newport.

back ride ($85 per person) from **Pisgah Forest Stables** (☎ 828-883-8258; 1hr/2hr $25/50; ☾ 10am, 11am, noon, 2pm, 3pm & 4pm). It's located on US 276 near Brevard.

GRAVEYARD FIELDS

Map 6; MP 418.8

There's nothing spooky about Graveyard Fields, unless you count the crowds in fall. A moderate hike leaves from here, and if you don't mind a few staircases, the only thing that'll jump out at you are three spectacular waterfalls.

From the parking lot, you'll notice a burned area of foliage down below the overlook. A massive fire in 1925 raged through this valley, catching more than 200 trout fishermen by surprise and trapping them. They survived by jumping into the Yellowstone prong, waiting underwater and taking small gulps of air amid the flames. When it was all over, the area's burnt-out stumps left a landscape resembling a 'field of tombstones,' hence the name.

WATERFALLS IN GRAVEYARD FIELDS HIKE (MP 418.8)

Start this moderate 0.8-mile hike by taking the stone steps at the Graveyard Fields Overlook down through a thick spread of rhododendrons and across a small streambed. The path can be a bit muddy due to heavy traffic and/or recent rainfall. **Yellowstone Waterfall** is the first waterfall you'll encounter after you cross the Yellowstone Prong of the Pigeon River. Just a few steps down from the wooden observation platform, you'll feel the mist from the falls.

Heading back, you can choose to return to the parking lot, or stay straight for a moderate 3.2-mile hike to **Upper Yellowstone Falls**. The trail climbs a little here among more picture-worthy clusters of rhododendrons as you hike away from the river. You'll know you're getting close to the falls when small stones turn to boulders and the sound of water grows louder.

Unique to this particular trail is the sheer number of wild berry bushes (blueberry, blackberry and gooseberry); they make good snacks for hikers and deer.

ON THE ROAD

From Graveyard Fields, the Parkway climbs steadily for the next 4 miles. A Cherokee legend claims that the devil holds court up in the caves you can see from the **Devils Courthouse Overlook** (MP 422.4) – hence the name – and some say that the craggy summit looks downright menacing. Regardless, it's a magnificent vista, and a lovely short hike yields even better, 360° views of the devilish formations.

Less than 10 miles later, you'll come to **Richland Balsam** (MP 431). Look for shutterbugs snapping photos in front of the sign that states this is 'the highest point of the Parkway,' at 6047ft. A moderate, 1.5-mile self-guided nature hike from the overlook loops through a disappearing spruce and fir forest.

A wonderful escape up a mountaintop drive, the luxurious **Balsam Mountain Inn** (MP 443; ☎ 800-224-9498, 828-456-9498; www.balsaminn.com; d $125-175) hangs onto down-home charm with a fireplace in the lobby, clapboards, sprawling porches and a very good restaurant. Rooms come without phones or TVs, but the inn offers an alternative diversion: regular shows of Appalachian art. To get there, from MP 443 take US 74/23.

WATERROCK KNOB

Map 6; MP 451.2

Its ethereal location perched at the top of the mountain makes Waterrock one of the most unique visitor centers. A 0.5-mile hiking trail leads to the knob and a 360° view of the Smoky Mountains – what the sign doesn't tell you is that it's a steep, rocky, uphill climb the entire way. Don't forget to pick up your certificate for climbing the knob – kids love the proof of their accomplishment.

WATERROCK KNOB TRAIL

This might be the hardest half mile you ever walk. But the extremely steep hike to the pedestrian overlook is absolutely worth the burn, and yes, there are plenty of benches along the way.

Start out from the visitor center parking lot, which is an ethereal experience itself when the fog rolls in. Walk up the paved path (with handrail) until it ends at rocky ground, and push on until you hit the pedestrian overlook, about a quarter mile from the parking lot. Catch your breath and take a few snaps here before climbing further, where it gets even rockier for a few hundred feet. Soon the trail opens up, and the terrain looks meadowlike – despite being 6000ft in the air. Speaking of which, if you're feeling lightheaded, it's only natural. Some hikers experience a bit of altitude sickness because of the sudden shift in elevation.

At the peak, you'll view the Great Smokies in Tennessee, as well as peaks in North Carolina, South Carolina and Georgia. You can even see the Ghost Town in the Sky amusement park down in Maggie Valley. A perfectly placed bench makes for a nice sunset seat. It's downhill all the way back...just watch out for those bears.

QUALLA BOUNDARY CHEROKEE RESERVATION

Map 6; MP 456

At **Soco Gap** (MP 456) the Parkway enters the Qualla Boundary Cherokee Reservation, lands held in federal trust by the Eastern Band of the Cherokee Indians. Soco Gap was known as the 'ambush place' (from the Cherokee word *ahaluna*) because it represented the entrance to Cherokee land from the north and east in the 1700s. In 1811 Soco Gap was the scene of a fateful council between Shawnee chief Tecumseh and Cherokee chief Junaluska, when Junaluska refused a proposal that the two tribes combine forces to fight the white settlers.

The Native Americans living here today trace their lineage to about 1000 individuals who eluded capture by federal agents during the forced relocation of the Cherokee to Oklahoma in 1838. Today the Qualla Boundary Cherokee Reservation is comprised of 56,688 acres. Towns include Big Cove, Birdtown, Paintown, Snowbird, Wolftown and Yellowhill, but most visitors only visit Cherokee, the largest North Carolina gateway town to the Great Smoky Mountains National Park.

NC 19 crosses the Parkway here; Cherokee is 8 miles west, and Maggie Valley is 3 miles east. If you are planning to visit Cherokee, see Lonely Planet's *Great Smoky Mountains & Shenandoah National Parks* for more information.

ON THE ROAD

Further ahead, **Lickstone Ridge** (5150ft) rises from below into a broad, flat-topped mountain running roughly southwest. The Lickstone Ridge Overlook (MP 459) provides a panoramic view of most of the Qualla Boundary, and the **Lickstone Ridge Tunnel** distinguishes itself by making a 45° turn inside the mountain.

At MP 461 are **Big Witch Gap** and **Big Witch Tunnel**, named for the Cherokee medicine man Tskil-e-gwa, also known as 'Big Witch.' At the time of his death in 1897, Big Witch was the eldest man of the tribe and the only one who could remember the Creek War of 1812–14. A skilled medicine man and herbalist, he was revered also for knowing how to kill an eagle so that its feathers could be used for sacred ceremonies.

At **Big Witch Overlook** (4160ft), you'll find appealing picnic tables with an excellent view overlooking the Qualla Boundary.

END OF THE BLUE RIDGE PARKWAY

You'll find no grand 'Congratulations! You did it!' at the end of this 469-mile journey. The Blue Ridge Parkway ends rather unceremoniously at the junction with US 441, just south of the entrance to Great Smoky Mountains National Park and at the northern edge of the town of Cherokee. But overused brake pads and sore hikers' knees aside, you can rest on your laurels for completing this incredible drive, hopefully with many snapshots along the way. Or, if you're up for more exploring, continue south into the Great Smoky Mountains National Park and discover why it's the most popular national park in the US. Pick up a copy of Lonely Planet's *Great Smoky Mountains & Shenandoah National Parks* to help you explore its wild boundaries.

INDEX